MACMILLAN MODERN DRAMATISTS

Macmillan Modern Dramatists
Series Editors: *Bruce King* and *Adele King*

Published titles

Reed Anderson, *Federico Garcia Lorca*
Eugene Benson, *J. M. Synge*
Renate Benson, *German Expressionist Drama*
Normand Berlin, *Eugene O'Neill*
Michael Billington, *Alan Ayckbourn*
John Bull, *New British Political Dramatists*
Denis Calandra, *New German Dramatists*
Neil Carson, *Arthur Miller*
Maurice Charney, *Joe Orton*
Ruby Cohn, *New American Dramatists, 1960–1980*
Bernard F Dukore, *American Dramatists, 1918–1945*
Bernard F Dukore, *Harold Pinter*
Arthur Ganz, *George Bernard Shaw*
Frances Gray, *John Arden*
Julian Hilton, *Georg Büchner*
David L Hirst, *Edward Bond*
Helene Keyssar, *Feminist Theatre*
Bettina L Knapp, *French Theatre 1918–1939*
Charles Lyons, *Samuel Beckett*
Susan Bassnett-McGuire, *Luigi Pirandello*
Margery Morgan, *August Strindberg*
Leonard C. Pronko, *Eugène Labiche and Georges Feydeau*
Jeanette L Savona, *Jean Genet*
Claude Schumacher, *Alfred Jarry and Guillaume Apollinaire*
Laurence Senelick, *Anton Chekhov*
Theodore Shank, *American Alternative Theatre*
James Simmons, *Sean O'Casey*
David Thomas, *Henrik Ibsen*
Dennis Walder, *Athol Fugard*
Thomas Whitaker, *Tom Stoppard*
Nick Worrall, *Nikolai Gogol and Ivan Turgenev*
Katharine Worth, *Oscar Wilde*

Further titles in preparation

MACMILLAN MODERN DRAMATISTS

EDWARD BOND

David L. Hirst
Lecturer in Drama,
University of Birmingham

M
MACMILLAN

First published 1985

Published by Higher and Further Education Division
MACMILLAN PUBLISHERS LTD
Houndmills, Basingstoke, Hampshire RG21 2XS
and London
Companies and representatives
throughout the world

Typeset by Type Generation Ltd,
London EC1

Printed in Hong Kong

British Library Cataloguing in Publication Data

Hirst, David L. 1942-
    Edward Bond. — (Macmillan modern dramatists)
    1. Bond, Edward — Criticism and interpretation
    I. Title
    822'.94   PR6052.05Z/

    ISBN 0–333–32030–1
    ISBN 0–333–32032–8 Pbk

Contents

List of Plates

Editors' Preface

The *Macmillan Modern Dramatists* is an international series of introductions to major and significant nineteenth and twentieth century dramatists, movements and new forms of drama in Europe, Great Britain, America and new nations such as Nigeria and Trinidad. Besides new studies of great and influential dramatists of the past, the series includes volumes on contemporary authors, recent trends in the theatre and on many dramatists, such as writers of farce, who have created theatre 'classics' while being neglected by literary criticism. The volumes in the series devoted to individual dramatists include a biography, a survey of the plays, and detailed analysis of the most significant plays, along with discussion, where relevant, of the political, social, historical and theatrical context. The authors of the volumes, who are involved with theatre as playwrights, directors, actors, teachers, and critics, are concerned with the plays as theatré and discuss such matters as performance, character interpretation and staging, along with themes and contexts.

BRUCE KING
ADELE KING

Acknowledgements

I would like to thank Edward Bond and Elizabeth Bond for their generous help and advice and Nick Philippou who co-directed *Early Morning* with me and himself directed the premiere of *The Tin Can People*. I am grateful to John C. Lindley and David M. Wynn whose kindness and hospitality facilitated the writing of the book.

The author and publishers are grateful to Associated Book Publishers for permission to quote extracts from the works of Edward Bond.

1
Points of Departure

On Music
Music cannot ask questions
It can startle
That is as good as a question

Music cannot give answers
It can persuade
That is as good as the truth
Music is very dangerous

(We are afraid to believe anything
 Scepticism is polite
  Conviction leads to argument
   Truth loses something if told)

At Auschwitz they hanged men to waltzes
In Chile they broke a musician's hands
With the same irony the church
Once took away heretics' tongues

So there must be a new music
A music you can't hang men to
A music that stops you breaking musicians' hands

'On Music' (*Theatre Poems and Songs* p. 78)

1

Edward Bond

July 12th 1976 saw the world premiere of a new work at the Royal Opera House, Covent Garden and the first performance of a modernised Jacobean classic at the Old Vic, London. The libretto of the former and the adaptation of the latter were the work of Edward Bond. Both the dramatic genres of these two pieces and the theatres in which they were performed – two of the oldest and most revered cultural establishments in Britain – may seem at variance with the revolutionary ideals of the writer who first came to prominence in the controversy surrounding his play *Saved* in 1965 and who is now a most intransigent critic of bourgeois capitalist values. How, it may be argued, could an artist committed to changing society in advocating the abolition of social and economic privilege, possibly concern himself with such an arcane dramatic form as opera or with re-writing an extravagant blood-boltered revenge tragedy? Ought not the responsible socialist artist to be involved with the working class and the traditions and theatrical venues appropriate to a marxist culture? Is it not the duty of the writer conscientiously furthering a social revolution to devote himself whole-heartedly to this end by living with the class he wishes to promote and by employing his talents to inspire and educate them?

The task for the responsible dramatist in Britain has never been more difficult or demanding then it is at present. The theatrical artist finds himself working in a political and cultural vacuum. Britain's self-awareness was once its strength. During the late sixteenth and early seventeenth centuries it encouraged a spirit of enquiry and discovery which absorbed the ideas of the Renaissance from the rest of Europe, resulting in a rich dramatic and cultural tradition. The elitism of Restoration theatre-going brought about a split between popular and literary drama which widened in the eighteenth century and was complete by the end of the nineteenth. In the present century it seemed at first that the verbally sophisticated, dramatically atrophied bourgeois theatre of the inter-war period had been destroyed completely by the radically new subject matter and form of the plays initially pioneered by the Royal Court in the mid 'fifties. Social environment changed, economic and political issues were aired, the well-made play gave way to absurdist drama, epic narrative and the Theatre of Cruelty. But the influence of such original writers as Beckett, Artaud and Brecht was short-lived in Britain. Beckett's excoriatory analysis was replaced by the whimsy of N. F. Simpson and the linguistic affectation of Stoppard, talents far more attractive to the British temperament. Both Charles Marowitz and Peter Brook, pioneers of the Theatre of Cruelty season in 1964, have found Britain an uncongenial place to work and have carried on their researches elsewhere. And the two most notable writers of the new dramatic movement, Pinter and Osborne, have been absorbed into the establishment. Pinter has moved from a genuinely disturbing social comedy of menace to a more refined and mollifying comedy of manners, whilst Osborne, the rebel of the 'fifties, having enjoyed success, has lost his bite.

The dramas of Pinter and Osborne have a psychological basis and are little concerned with social and political ethics beyond a narrowly prescribed area. They are significantly two of Britain's most highly-regarded post-war dramatists precisely because the British theatre encourages and prefers this emphasis. Brecht has had as little effect in Britain as Marx. There is no tradition of political theatre in his epic style any more than there is an effective communist party. This sets Britain firmly apart not only from eastern European countries, but also from France, Italy and Germany. Artists such as Dario Fo, Roger Planchon,

Joachim Herz or Gotz Friedrich operate within a recognisable Marxist culture which not only gives a purpose to their work, but also enables them to employ techniques from popular and epic theatre in contexts as diverse as the circus tent and the opera house. Such figures are quite alien to the British theatrical scene. Even as guests working in British theatres and opera houses they have become progesssively more unwelcome. For the political dramatist in Britain the situation is even more critical.

Bond would endorse the opinion of Ben Jonson, a figure to whom he gave vivid and sympathetic theatrical life in *Bingo* (1973): 'The ends of all who for the scene do write. Are – or should be – to profit and delight'. The hesitation in the parenthesis is as significant as the order of the two infinitives. Jonson was a most powerful dramatic critic of contemporary bourgeois values, a social satirist skilled at ridiculing the mercenary ethic of the city, clear-sighted and unromantic in his approach. He is the perfect foil to Shakespeare both in real life and in the opening scene of the second act of Bond's play. Here he forces Shakespeare to evaluate his later dramas, making him ask: 'Was anything done?', a question as to whether the dramatist has fulfilled his ethical function. For Bond the demands are more extreme. He is committed to exposing a system rather than attacking abuses, which was essentially the purpose of Jonson's satire. In dramas with a contemporary setting from *Saved* (1965) through to *The Worlds* (1979) Bond has exposed the corruption and insanity of a world founded on capitalism. As he has developed his dramatic skills and political philosophy he has moved from a presentation of the situation through to a demonstration of how to change it. His Marxism is more fundamental, however, in that it informs his concern with the inter-relation of past, present and future. In his plays he has constantly turned to crucial periods in the history of the world, to examine the social, ethical and political roots of present situations in order to alter them in the future. His concern both with the responsibility of the artist and his relationship to his time informs not only *Bingo* but also *The Fool* (1975) as well as *Narrow Road To The Deep North* (1968) and its companion piece, *The Bundle* (1978). Victorian and Edwardian values are examined respectively in *Early Morning* (1968) and *The Sea* (1973) whilst *Human Cannon* explores the ethics of revolution in the setting of the Spanish Civil War.

Bond is equally concerned with the relationship of dramatic form to social conditions and historical evolution. This is particularly significant for the contemporary writer in Britain. The founder of Italian communism, Antonio Gramsci, argued that without a knowledge of the past it was impossible to understand the present and make any advances. This opinion is voiced by Gramsci in a play by Dario Fo: *The Worker Knows 300 Words, The Boss 1000; That's Why He's The Boss* (1969), which is a critical exploration of the history of communism in Italy. Fo is an interesting counterpart to Bond as a committed Marxist writer. His play is both set in and was first performed at a *Casa del Popolo*, a worker's club. It contains dramatisation of Stalinist trials and Mafia murder, culminating in the recreation of a Mayakovsky dance drama. Gradually Fo has moved from traditional theatre (as a 'jester of the bourgeoisie') through Communist Party venues to warehouses, abandoned palaces and circus tents. He plays regularly to as many as two thousand people. His plays draw on epic techniques as well as improvised *commedia* clowning: the traditions are as familiar to his audiences as are the historical and political issues which they relish. He is working within a popular dramatic medium which is the expression of a marxist culture. The political writer in

England is unable to do this. There is no Marxist culture and there is no popular dramatic medium capable of conveying sophisticated social and political ideas.

The choices that face the British writer are different. He can, like Trevor Griffiths, conclude that the only popular medium of any significance is television and write essentially for this, hoping in effect to subvert the ideas of his mass audience. Or he can, like Wesker and Joan Littlewood attempt to create something along the lines of a 'Fun Palace': a rendezvous for working-class people where they enjoy undemanding, non high-brow entertainment. Or, he can choose the path of John Arden and Margaretta D'Arcy and work with a particular group of oppressed people, informing them through parables and stories cast in the popular idiom of music hall and melodrama. Another possibility is to operate on the Fringe, speaking of necessity to a limited number but employing techniques of radical political theatre to attack the establishment and advocate alternative policies. The dangers inherent in these diverse courses of action point to the basic inability of British theatre to establish any relationship between vital popular theatrical conventions and political education. Of the choices, Griffith's decision may seem the most useful and honest. The various theatrical alternatives are scarcely satisfactory. There is a danger of patronising a working-class audience by assuming the only culture to which they can relate is one of beer and skittles, an attitude Fo for one is deeply contemptuous of. Or lack of critical objectivity can lead to the danger of romanticising concepts such as the Irish rebel hero. Moreover melodrama and music hall are dead forms; they are not adequate media for conveying a thoughtful political message unless subjected to the ironic perspective of a writer such as Peter Nichols. The danger of preaching to the converted or talking to yourself is also one into which the English Fringe has more increasingly fallen. For oppressed minority groups, be it blacks, gays or women, to write plays themselves about themselves for themselves may be both narcissitic and reactionary. Bond had precisely the right idea when asked by Gay Sweatshop to write a play for them. He produced a powerful parable about the nature of oppression and the inter-relation of social and political forces which made no explicit reference to homosexuality.

Bond has chosen a path very different from the politically-committed writers and artists discussed above. His handling of dramatic techniques mirrors precisely his treatment of social and political structures. Just as he sees it necessary to understand the history of Britain's social and political institutions in order to change them, so too he has progressively come to realize that as particular dramatic genres are representative of ideas and ideals of their time, it is by coming to terms with them and adapting them that the responsible playwright can most effectively operate. The witty comedy of manners, an invention of the post-Restoration dramatists was the vehicle for expressing their particular ethical and social values. In *Restoration* (1981) Bond treats this style as a basis on which he can superimpose his own very different viewpoint. The most composite dramatic exploration of the moral and psychological concerns of the late nineteenth century bourgeoisie was the naturalistic tragi-comedy. In *Summer* (1982) Bond employs the obsession with the past characteristic of Ibsen in the context of a naturalistic Chekovian drama to expose Britain's far more disturbing post-war political inheritance. The tragedy of fifth-century B.C. Athens as it had developed by the time of Euripides to encompass more epic concerns and concomitant stage devices is a mirror reflecting the state of a nation at a crucial point in its history. In

The Woman (1978) Bond skilfully reworks *The Trojan Women* so as to cast the image of that society into the present and inform contemporary political opinion.

These dramatic strategies are a comparatively recent part of his development as a playwright, but they are a logical extension of that acute concern with dramatic form which made him create plays as different as *Early Morning* and *Narrow Road To The Deep North* straight after his first more conventionally realistic pieces, *The Pope's Wedding* (1962) and *Saved*. He feels the need to go beyond the exposition of contemporary social evils to an indication of a more positive means of remedying them, and this added sense of responsibility brings with it an increased awareness that the dramatic medium in which he is operating needs to be equally sophisticated. Bleak social realism in the theatrical style pioneered by the Royal Court can be a perfectly adequate vehicle for painting life as it is. Even though in *Saved* Bond's realism was not merely of the surface, he only pointed the way tentatively to a better life. Now he feels committed to showing precisely how this may be brought about, and thus the dramatic devices he employs have grown more expressive and dynamic. In selecting different theatrical stylisations from the past which are reflective of the ethics of specific historical periods and in combining them with his own original techniques, Bond has established himself as the leading pioneer of political theatre.

A consideration of this approach enables us to see more clearly the significance of the opera *We Come to the River* and the adaptation of *The White Devil* in the development of Bond's work. Neither of these pieces has received much consideration by previous critics, yet they are important in Bond's output since they represent an attempt to speak to a different audience from that which had attended his previous dramas, and because the period of their composition and date of their first performance marks a watershed in his career. Prior to 1976 his plays had been almost exclusively written for and performed at the Royal Court. After this he was to create only one play for the English Stage Company: *Restoration*. The break with the establishment which had nurtured his talents was a crucial one; it was a reflection of his own development as a dramatist as well as a corollary of the changing face of the British avant-garde theatre. *We Come To The River* and *The White Devil* do not represent Bond at his most extended since he was only a collaborator in both, but they are a useful starting point since they show us very clearly his conception of theatre both in his attitude to the audience and his basic methods of composition.

'We Come To The River'

Bond and the German composer of the opera, Hans Werner Henze have a great deal in common. Henze is a committed Marxist who has worked out the implications of his political convictions in the development of his original musical style. Having left Germany after the war he settled in Italy where the influence of Italian culture – both musical and political – influenced the style of his writing. Like Bond he has worked through traditional forms – in his case symphony, concerto, oratorio, opera – transforming them to his own ends. After his opera *The Bassarids* (1966) with a libretto by W.H. Auden and Chester Kallman based on *The Bacchae* of Euripides his music took on a harsher, more aggressively polemical tone. The meeting with Bond proved crucial to the further development of both artists.

Edward Bond

Henze has commented:

> Edward Bond described his libretto as 'Actions for music' and in fact his libretto and the actions it contains are, in many respects inconceivable as a stage play: everything that takes place – and the way in which it takes place – is aimed at music. You have to go a step further and say aimed at *my* music, namely to demand of it something that it had hitherto refused to provide. For until my meeting and debate with him I had thought that it was possible for music to adopt a passive attitude towards contemporary reality, one of the most striking phenomena of which is violence, and thereby to retreat from it into abstraction, or react merely with songs of lamenatation or accusation.

> (Music and Politics: p. 231.)

This 'passive attitude towards contemporary reality' is precisely what Bond has opposed from his first play; he has no time for playwrights who refuse to meet the challenge of attempting to answer the social and political problems of their age.

Bond and Henze produced a work which operates within a traditional framework of recognisable techniques: instead of creating an avant-garde music-theatre piece, rejecting operatic conventions, or a play with musical commentary, they effected an original synthesis of drama and music. Their approach is clear-cut; though Bond's theatrical language is unusual and Henze's musical idiom harmonically advanced, they tell their story with absolute clarity and telling force. The seasoned opera-goer who appreciates Berg or Britten would understand it, but so would a musically untrained mind receptive to the words and the sounds.

It is worth considering the audience this work is aimed at.

Because of the high price of opera going in England and the misplacement of subsidy which encourages *ad hoc* perform-ances by expensive international singers, a company work of this sort – with a cast of over a hundred – has to be rehearsed in very different conditions from those governing the average opera in the Covent Garden repertoire. It has never been revived there, though it has been frequently performed in Europe. Clearly a more enquiring audience would attend such a piece than would be drawn to *Madam Butterfly* or *The Barber of Seville*. By reducing seat prices and introducing ticket concessions a substantially younger audience was encouraged to visit the Royal Opera House. What precisely was the intention of the creators then, in presenting the work to such an audience?

Their aim – as expressed in a joint programme note – might at first seem a far cry from their achievement, since the context would appear to circumscribe their avowed intentions and compromise them totally. Bond and Henze stated:

> The opera house may seem remote from the street. But art isn't an ego strip-tease in an ivory tower. The nature of art in our times is controlled by the man in the street, and it's he who defines the responsibility of the artist – *not* through an act of goodwill or condescension by the artist, but because art *can* now only be created by struggling to portray and understand the problems of the street. The artist must show people, related to their society and time, in such a way that they are given the reassurance of the rationality which is at the centre of art.

The last sentence expressed a concept absolutely fun-damental to Bond's work: his belief in a 'rational theatre'

11

which will tell the truth clearly and thus inform the audience how to effect change.

Of course Bond and Henze did not expect their audience to rush out of the theatre prepared to begin the Revolution. Bond is sceptical of the value of any immediate effect a theatrical performance may have on the spectator. How he or she feels and thinks six months later is far more important. They may have resented what they saw or argued with it, but later they may well recognise the truth of what they at first rejected. The reverse is equally true: an intense feeling of compassion or anger soon disperses. The audience need to have their thought-patterns changed, not their emotions aroused. The scope of Bond's intentions is a wide one. He knows society will not be changed overnight – and certainly not by the theatre. What the dramatist can do – *must* do – however, is to reject outmoded concepts of authority and justice, and create instead new standards and a new morality. This is more succinctly expressed in the Covent Garden programme note than anywhere else in Bond's writing:

. . . the art of an age is defined by the politics of that age. In the past art helped to create the images of Pharoah, Ceasar, the King, aristocrats and merchants. In doing so it helped to create human consciousness in those ages. It provided images, music, description, in which those societies could recognise themselves. In our age the artist must help to create the image and consciousness of the working class. There *is* nothing else art can do now, that is the definition of art in our time.

This does not imply that the artist must write exclusively *about* and *for* the working class. At least not in the short term. To do so can all too easily lead to what Bond and

Henze call 'goodwill' and 'condescension'. The artist should not compromise or vulgarise the medium in which he is working by spurious attempts at writing in a popular idiom. Moreover this would mean he was essentially speaking to the converted, or worse still, trying to convert the working man to his own higher view of his destiny. You will not change society by addressing yourself exclusively to the man in the street. You must influence the views of a wider cross-section of the public; you must educate – or re-educate – those who will have power, either because they are given it or because they seize it. It is vital to understand Bond's stance in this matter or we can too easily be confused by very different criteria of what constitutes valid political theatre. The extreme example of an opera about working-class struggle against imperialism furnishes us with the clearest explanation of the apparent contradiction inherent in the difference between Bond's subject matter and his audience.

Bond provided Henze with a picture of 'the weak and the poor whose vulnerability changes into strength and becomes a force that changes the world' (*Music and Politics* p. 232). Henze saw the clearest contemporary example of this as Vietnam, where, after thirty years of war a people succeeded in freeing themselves from an imperialist superpower. He also describes the historical facts which influenced the portrayal of the opposite side. Refugees from the fascist dictatorship in Chile told of 'the murder squads, the concentration camps, torture, fear, about all the repression that had been inflicted with icy, murderous coldness on people on whom the fascists were now venting their anger simply because they had taken a step towards national independence, renewal and socialism, and in a few years had shaken the forces of reaction to their foundations.' (*op. cit.* p. 233) The immediacy of the opera is one of its most striking features: it is present in the series of monologues Bond gives to the madmen in scene thirteen (a horrific catalogue of atrocities encompassing the Nazi death camps and the bombing of Hiroshima), as well as in the details of the narrative itself. This is matched by the directness and force of Henze's music. The story unfolds in an imaginary empire. A general, after winning a gruelling military campaign, is informed that he will – as the result of an old injury – eventually lose his sight. This makes him look with new sympathy on the suffering of the victims of war and forces him to renounce publicly the violence he once unquestioningly accepted. He is confined in a madhouse. Yet he refuses to take a political stand: he will not support a soldier who urges him to lead a revolt of the oppressed, and he rejects the role of popular hero which would lend credence to the Emperor's regime. The soldier assassinates the Governor and the Emperor has the General blinded. The doctor's grimly mysterious prophesy has been realised. The General now sees more clearly the victims of the war who appear to him and sing of their hope for a better future. Simultaneously the madmen, not comprehending this, murder him.

The subject of *We Come To The River*, though unusual, is not without precedent in the operatic repertoire. Berg's *Wozzeck* (1925), an adaptation of Büchner's play, ennobles the poor soldier who is obliged through economic pressures to submit himself to medical experiments and who is driven to murder and finally suicide. Closer to the Bond-Henze work is Zimmerman's *Die Soldaten* (1960), an adaptation of another German classic: Lenz's drama of military and class oppression. Henze's music has affinities with the advanced idiom Zimmerman uses and it is interesting that *Die Soldaten* also employs simultaneous action on three stages; but if Bond's libretto owes anything

14

to Zimmerman in this respect it is quite different in a more fundamental way. What is so original about *We Come To The River* is not that it is the first proletarian opera – the *verismo* school in late nineteenth century Italy set a vogue for down-beat working-class settings – but that it is the first opera to present a successful class struggle against imperialism. Though this victory is only of dead victims whose ghosts ultimately triumph – a recurrent theme in Bond's drama, – it is in marked contrast to the tragic despair with which Zimmerman's opera concludes and which precipitated his own suicide. In *We Come To The River* Henze and Bond are forging a powerful new image of the working-class and enforcing it on the mind of a middle class audience in order to modify their social and political consciousness.

The opera encapsulates many of the key themes in Bond's work. The tyranny of an unjust regime is familiar from *Early Morning* and *Lear* (1971) and will recur in *The Bundle* and *The Woman*. The search for truth and the enlightment which comes through suffering are also central concepts in *Early Morning* and *Lear*, whilst the metaphor of blinding further extends the paradox from Shakespeare's play expressed in Gloucester's comment 'I stumbled when I saw'. Madness is also a theme of *Early Morning*, most fully dramatised in the final scene of *The Fool*, and recurring in *The Worlds*. In the opera we witness for the first time Bond's extended vision of the better life. It comes at the end as the dead victims sing:

> We stand by the river
> If there is no bridge we will wade
> If the water is deep we will swim
> If it is too fast we will build boats
> We will stand on the other side
> We have learnt to march so well that we cannot drown.
> (op. cit. p. 122)

This climactic song will become the central issue of *The Bundle*, *The Worlds* and *Human Cannon* (1985) which are concerned with realising this better life through revolution. The opera enabled Bond to write what is in effect a poetic parable rather than a play. It is a form at which he excels and it enables the work to function dramatically through techniques which may at first seem restricted to music theatre but which Bond has subsequently learned to adapt also to the ends of his own drama.

The combination of music and drama can effect a particularly rich and complex theatrical structure. Music drama – whether more traditional opera or more recent experiments in the mixed media – is the natural successor of poetic drama. Precisely because Verdi and Wagner realised the potential of a more vital theatrical form than that achieved by romantic poets and dramatists it is to the opera house that we must turn for the richest and most significant contributions to theatre in the late nineteenth and early twentieth century. Bond's drama has always been deeply poetic. It is to his images – verbal and physical – and to their precision of complex orchestration that we should look for the true poetic drama of today, rather than to the minimalist utterances of Beckett and Pinter or the rhetoric of Osborne and Stoppard. In Bond's economy of style coupled with the breadth of his imagination we can appreciate the stage poet. In the more conventional sense of the word he is a writer of poetry too, as the lengthy volume *Theatre Poems and Songs* illustrates. All of these pieces – whether written for inclusion in his plays or as explanations and further illustrations of his ideas – reveal that Bond conceives his dramas in terms of images, not words, and in the organising of these images his plays take on musical affinities. For this reason his dramas yield only a fraction of their quality in reading; only by experiencing them in performance does the full richness of their texture make itself felt.

Just as Henze through his collaboration with Bond learned how to move away from the abstraction he had previously felt intrinsic to the musical idiom and ground his composition in a genuine immediacy and reality, so Bond acquired from his experience of working on the opera a new awareness of how to achieve a more complex dramatic language which could portray with greater richness and subtlety his vision of the revolutionary change necessary within society. Together the two of them created a musical and theatrical language capable of presenting both the reality of political oppression and the basis of a new society with a directness and force which avoids the two extremes of the sentimental and the prosaic. The work demands a space that produces the illusion of three different stages, each of which is allotted a small instrumental ensemble which plays only when the action is on that stage. These ensembles are contrasted, the nature of the musical accompaniment thus reflecting the different dramatic contexts: Stage I in the foreground is primarily used for monologues and depicts the world of the oppressed; the central scenes take place on Stage II; whilst Stage III, deep in the background, is the scene of the terrible attrocities.

This disposition of the spaces lends to some telling ironic effects. The simultaneous action of scenes 4, 5 and 6 means that while army officers are waltzing with whores on the back stage, the Doctor is telling the General he will go blind (to an orchestral *chaconne*) centre stage, and meanwhile on the forestage a deserter is awaiting execution (to music marked 'with extreme anguish'). As the Doctor pronounces the word 'blind', the Deserter 'touches his forehead' and says: 'Shoot here.' The next sequence takes this further. As the parade ground is swept on Stage I at the command of a

Sergeant Major who sings an elaborately comic *coloratura* routine, a woman, searching for her husband's body on the Battlefield (Stage II) thinks she has found him; he is in fact being shot as a deserter (on Stage III). But the music on this upper stage has not changed since the previous scene; the ensemble continues to play dance music: a waltz. Henze comments: 'Thus a feeling of powerlessness is expressed at the same horrifying image of the camp orchestra at Auschwitz, which by order of the commandant had to play at executions.' This rich dramatic texture is nevertheless immediately appreciable to the audience; powerful and disturbing ethical and political points have been made through a familiar musical and theatrical medium handled with great originality. After his collaboration with Henze Bond's work took on an added poetic and musical depth to match the advance in Henze's writing which the latter refers to when he adds: 'Perhaps this is one of the clearest illustrations of what I had in mind when I said that in this work music has been brought to a level of realism that I would have avoided in the past. Here violence is itself portrayed by means of an act of violence'. (*Music and Politics* p. 239).

Similarly the presentation of faith in the future is given a force and complexity through essentially musical means. Bond provides a characteristic complexity through the paradox of the final 'drowning' of the General by the madmen counterpointed with the triumphant song of the victims. This is in itself a poetic, indeed musical, technique. Henze expands it by his handling of the music associated with the oppressed. Whilst the material relating to the world of violence – 'the sound of orchestra III', he states, 'has something altogether vulgar, belching, repellent and sarcastic about it' – gradually becomes stiff and dies, the material associated with the oppressed develops and grows.

He gives a series of musical fragments to the Deserter, his Mother, the Young Woman, Soldier II and his Wife; these are repeated throughout the work and then in the final song 'they form a chain of intervals which is a metaphor for hope, a hope for love and peace that is possible only now at the end of the opera. All fear and anxiety have left the music; the end is like a new beginning in a world freed from terror and injustice'. (*op. cit.* p. 242).

'The White Devil'

The same day that *We Come To The River* was premiered, Bond's version of Webster's *The White Devil* opened at the Old Vic. It is intriguing that Bond should have been drawn to this play, one of the most extravagantly baroque examples of the Jacobean revenge drama or tragedy of blood. There are two immediate reasons for his interest in the piece: his concern with the theme of violence, and his fascination with the drama of the early seventeenth century. He had already written *Lear* and his study of Shakespeare's despairing end, *Bingo*, as well as an adaptation of Middleton's comedy of Jacobean citizen life: *A Chaste Maid in Cheapside* (1966). Nor did it come as too much of a surprise for the playwright who had presented such scenes of graphic violence as the stoning of the baby in *Saved*, the beating up of Len in *Early Morning* or the torturing of Warrington in *Lear* to turn his attention to the catalogue of refined murders which caused Shaw to dismiss Webster as a 'Tussaud laureate'. By the mid 'seventies Bond himself had earned in some quarters a reputation as a pornographer through his handling of violence on stage. Such a criticism is as shortsighted as Shaw's contemptuous dismissal of Webster. There are some marked parallels between the work of Shaw and Bond, and it is revealing at this point to consider the adaptation of *The White Devil*. It tells us as much about Bond's interests and dramatic technique as Shaw's intriguing rewrite of *Cymbeline* (as *Cymbeline Refinished*) – 'as though it were post Ibsen and not post Marlowe' – tells us about the moral and psychological concerns of another social and political dramatist.

The first thing that is observable in a comparison of Webster's play and Bond's adaptation is the added clarity of the latter. Literary critics have done their best to defend Webster's drama against the accusations of clumsy construction made most notably by William Archer at the end of the nineteenth century. The play makes a powerful impression on revival, but that the plot is notoriously difficult to follow on stage was borne out by a previous production by the National Theatre company at the Old Vic in 1970. Directed by Frank Dunlop and designed by Piero Gherardi, Fellini's assistant, this staging came over as an outrageous Renaissance fresco, almost entirely lacking in dramatic logic or motivation. Bond's version is by contrast crystal clear in its plotting from the start. This is achieved by very simple but effective means: by paring down the text and by the transference of a number of conversations crucial to the plotting to positions where they assume a sharper, more pointed theatrical focus. The character who is vital to the unfolding of the plot throughout is Lodovico, and there is a very real danger of him moving out of focus in Webster's play. After his explosive opening: 'Banished!' Webster then allows Lodovico to expatiate on the nature of Fortune for eleven lines. Bond cuts these to three and thus the phrase: 'Fortune's a right whore' makes its point the more powerfully. Later in the drama, after a prolonged absence Lodovico will return from banishment and avenge the murder of Isabella with whom he is secretly in love. Webster buries this information in Act II scene 2 where it is in danger of being lost. Bond transfers the relevent lines to the opening of Act III where they stand out in sharp contrast to the trial scene which follows. On the page this alteration may seem trivial, pointless even; in the theatre it makes a world of difference to our response. It is entirely characteristic of the dramatist who in *Early Morning* – a play which yields little of its meaning on reading – can guide us with absolute security through a labyrinthine plot by employing a series of clear *theatrical* signs which ensure that we are never in any danger of losing our way. Bond's adaptation of Webster's play serves to confirm his skill as the most powerful story-teller in the contemporary theatre.

The White Devil also tells us a great deal about Bond's social and political concerns. Again, through a subtle shift of emphasis, brought about not by altering lines but by changing the perspective of the audience, Bond draws our attention to implications beyond the merely personal and psychological. This is entirely consistent with the aims of the Marxist dramatist who sees Webster's play both in relation to its own time and as a reflection of the present. Bond has said: 'It's not about sexual violence and intense personal emotion, but power and money' (Hay and Roberts p. 218): a comment which, incidentally, could apply to *Saved*, *Lear* or *Bingo*.

The way Bond achieves this shift of focus can be seen most clearly from an examination of the last act. Here the emotional issues come to their climax, but are handled in such a way as to deflect our emotional sympathy. Cornelia, the innocent victim of the action, is most in danger of claiming our attention in Webster's play. Bond takes her mad scene (Act V scene iv), splits it into a number of short sections, and distributes these throughout the act. She remains on stage whilst the climactic events are unfolding, oblivious of them, a silent commentator whose brief outbursts serve as ineffective comments on a more politically important sequence of events. The murder of Bracciano is the crucial act, seen not so much as the final realisation of a psychological vendetta but rather as the most vital issue in the transference of power. For much of the lengthy death scene Bond keeps Brachiano off stage, his screaming and final desperation being the mere accompaniment to the more important action taking place on the stage. This is achieved by pointed stage directions:

> FLAMINEO goes through the doors into the state appartments. CORNELIA tends MARCELLO. BRACCIANO is heard screaming off. FRANCISCO, GASPARO, LODOVICO walk up and down, shaking with excitement, wringing their hands, gesticulating, miming satisfaction and pleasure to each other. There are silences between the calls from inside the State appartments. (5.2.14)

The final murder of Bracciano is expanded into a powerful image, a Brechtian Gestus paralleling that which sums up the escalating violence in Act 1 of *Lear* as the Gravedigger's Boy is shot whilst Cordelia is raped:

> They wind a longish scarf around his neck. They each take an end. Turn their backs on the duke, and strain as hard as they can – like two bookends facing away from each other. Then they remember to look over their shoulders and study the dying duke's grimaces. (5.2.19)

The simile of the bookends has all the force of a Jacobean conceit, giving clear physical definition to an action which has moved well beyond the sphere of the psychological.

The cuts in the text throughout this lengthy scene serve to increase the pace of the action and focus on the crucial issues, notably at the jarring shift of perspective occasioned by the editing of Lodovico's speech:

> He's fallen into a strange distraction.
> He talks of battles and monopolies,
> Levying of taxes, and from that descends
> To the most brain-sick language.
> He hath conferr'd the whole state of the dukedom
> Upon your sister, till the prince arrive
> At mature age. (5.2.13)

Bond's central concern – power – comes into the clearest focus here, and is emphasised by the stage direction which prefaces this conversation of Francisco and Flamineo:

> Exeunt all to State appartments except FLAMINEO, FRANCISCO AND CORNELIA. From time to time secretaries, officials, diplomats, nurses – all in strange uniforms and costumes, with official hats – rush through into the State appartments. The nurses carry medieval medical instruments and the secretaries, officials and diplomats carry documents and records – warrants, trade agreements, petitions, letters, to be seen and signed by the duke before he dies.' (5.2.12)

With this adaptation Bond took a classic and reworked it, playing down its literary and emotional characteristics in order to make it speak as a political commentary both on its own period and our own. In so doing he introduced a Marxist discipline into a firmly bourgeois context: the Old Vic theatre. *The White Devil* stands alongside *We Come To The River* as a neat indication of the tactic Bond has consistently employed throughout his dramatic career.

2
Theatres, Actors and Audiences

The stage does not go inside the mind as easily as novels and music can, but it can demonstrate social relationships between people more concretely than other arts. All theatre is political – Coward's as well as Brecht's – and theatre always emphasises the social in art. The audience judges in the same complex way that it judges in ordinary life. But it is given this advantage: it may look at things it would normally run from in fear, turn from in embarrassment, prevent in anger, or pass by because they are hidden, either purposefully or innocently. So audiences respond with all the faculties of their consciousness to the things that determine their social and private lives.

A Note On Dramatic Method p. xii-xiii

Bond has never had a play produced in a West End theatre. It may seem that such a situation is quite understandable when dealing with a politically-committed non-commercial dramatist, but Bond's relationship with the London theatrical scene is unique. He has seen his works performed at the Old Vic, The Royal Opera House and the National Theatre. His attitude is quite different from that of John Arden whose theatrical career has led him to work with and reject major establishment venues. John Arden's dissatisfaction with the London theatrical establishment – most acute in the renunciation of the Royal Shakespeare Company's production of *The Island of the Mighty* – has led to a self-imposed exile from England and a desire to involve himself with local communities. Bond works differently. He believes that only by taking on the establishment and extending the political debate in the most public of venues can bourgeois values be challenged and conventional patterns of thought changed. Moreover, the radical nature of this tactic can be gauged by the fact that, unlike Osborne's work, Bond's plays have never transferred to the commercial West End theatre. Osborne has never been more than a rebel; Bond is essentially a revolutionary. He wants to change the world and he will employ the most effective theatrical media to do so.

Bond, along with Arden and Osborne, is a product of the Royal Court Theatre, where in 1956, the English Stage Society inaugurated its policy of encouraging new dramatic talent. All three playwrights were discovered and nurtured there, but none of them now writes for that theatre. It is worth examining both when and why the Royal Court was such an important cultural centre and – more interestingly – why it is no longer so. The development – or decline – of the Royal Court in the last ten years crystallises the problem of the relationship between the political playwright and his audience, a problem which dramatists have attempted to solve in a variety of ways.

In 1966, the year after *Saved*, the Royal Court published an illustrated account of its first ten years. At the end of this George Goetschius, a social worker and research consultant for the London Council of Social Service, wrote a perceptive article: *The Royal Court in its Social Context* in which he discusses why the theatre had become a rallying point for social and political drama. He argues that as a result of social changes following the Second World War – with increased geographical, social, vocational and educational mobility – it was necessary to provide a place for a large number of people within the class structure of British society. This group was composed essentially of three elements: upper working class children of skilled artisans who were attempting to leave behind working class allegiances, lower middle class workers newly achieving success in the older professions and many new ones (in the media and industry), and a small number of middle and upper class people who wanted to break away from pre-war patterns (sons and daughters of colonial administrators, for example). He concludes:

> All three of these elements had in common the need to clear away part of the middle class way of life and to make the necessary psychological place within which to establish their new identity. This involved questioning the old identity and the social paraphernalia which surrounded it . . . The success of the Court I would attribute to its allowing itself after *Look Back* to become one of the rallying points for those elements in the middle class who were attempting to clear the social scene of what they saw to be some of its impediments and irrelevancies. In this sense the Court was a theatre of middle class transition. (*op. cit.* p. 33)

It is difficult to imagine how writers like Bond, Arden and Osborne could have made themselves heard in the climate of the British theatre prior to the revolutionary approach of the English Stage Society at the Royal Court. Bond, born into the lower working class, brought up in North London by parents who had come up to the city from East Anglia during the Depression because they were unable to get work on the land, submitted two plays to the Court in 1958. These were *Klaxon In Atreus' Palace* and *The Fiery Tree*, neither of which was performed but which led to him being invited to join the Writers' group at the Court and becoming a regular play-reader for the theatre. Four years later his first play was produced at the Court: *The Pope's Wedding*, given a single (Sunday night) performance without decor. On the strength of this the artistic director, George Devine, commissioned a new play. Two years later Bond submitted *Saved*, which was first performed in 1965, when the Court initiated a new regime after the retirement of Devine.

By the time *Saved* reached performance the Court had become established as a theatre 'of middle class transition.' In his article Goetschius goes on to question what the future of the theatre might be. He recognises the complacency which was setting in: observable in such phenomena as the respectability of the new professions, the decline in the Nuclear Disarmament movement and the emergence of films such as *Tom Jones* and *The Charge of the Light Brigade*. This was the 'swinging sixties' with its whole new pantheon of cultural idols and its pronouncedly liberal attitude to politics and morality. 'What perhaps is necessary' claimed Goetschius is:

a new Jimmy Porter who will give up the sweet stall, abandon some of his sexual obsessions and class-inflicted self-consciousness, and even the nostalgia of 'slim volumes of verse' and say something relevant to Britain in the 'sixties, a Britain which has moved so far beyond the angry young man and the kitchen sink as to give the impression that these were somehow involved in the Irish question and the Easter rebellion. (*op. cit.* p. 34)

Bond was to be this new voice and there is a resemblance between his explosion onto the theatrical scene and that of Osborne ten years previously. *Saved* – the play which was to produce every bit as much controversy as *Look Back In Anger* – was a far cry from the drama by then associated with the Court. Like *Look Back In Anger* it was produced in repertory with other plays expected to please the new middle class audience and support the risky venture of mounting a radically different piece by an unknown writer. In the first season in 1956 Osborne's play ran with works by established writers not previously associated with the theatre: Angus Wilson's *The Mulberry Bush* and Nigel Dennis's *Cards of Identity* as well as Arthur Miller's *The Crucible*. The English Stage Society repeated its mistake of relying on estabished authors – this time two Royal Court playwrights Ann Jellicoe and N. F. Simpson – whose dramas *Shelley* and *The Cresta Run* were mounted to prop up the novelty and daring of *Saved*. These two plays have met a similar fate to those of Angus Wilson and Nigel Dennis. There is a moral to be drawn from this, as Charles Marowitz pointed out in characteristically trenchant vein in 1966:

> Often I feel the Court is being run by half-witted, menopausic old crones with a possessive attachment to family ties and an irrational loathing for anyone not directly or indirectly traceable on the family tree. Then at other times I feel that only in such a swirling atmosphere of quirkiness and hypersensitivity could work of such a high calibre be produced. (*Confessions of a Counterfeit Critic* p. 113)

The Royal Court, in fact, has never had a policy beyond the celebrated and oft-quoted maxim of George Devine: 'the right to fail'. It might have appeared in 1965 that the new regime wished to initiate a firm line of approach by reinstating the repertory system and by a determination to integrate the work of the Court's experimental studio more directly with the productions mounted. But the artistic direction, divided between Gaskill, the director, John-stone, the head of the script department and studio, and Cuthbertson, an actor and director from the Glasgow Citizens Theatre, was from the start unstable. Shortly afterwards Gaskill took over effective control but then left to work with the more radical group, Joint Stock – a situation Bond has described as 'the Royal Court in exile'. The problem is clearly glimpsed in Johnstone's assertion:

> The lack of policy or at least a sign of a policy at certain stages was the theatre's greatest value when one looks back because of the extraordinary variety of work that was done: a French farce, *Happy Days*, a Brecht play, Keith Waterhouse and then a Genet. I wouldn't like us to get to the stage where you knew in advance the kind of play the Court would put on. (*Three At Court: Plays and Players* November 1965 p. 9)

Bond thinks differently. In *The Theatre I Want* which he wrote in 1981 for the publication *At the Royal Court*, a celebration of twenty-five years of the English Stage Company, he precisely instances this liberal aestheticism as a weakness:

> It seems to me that you cannot any longer create without socialism and that it is therefore not only nonsense to ask an actor to act in Beckett one night and in Brenton the

29

next – it is also nonsense to expect the audience to enjoy one and then the other. If they did, we have to say that they don't understand either . . . I think many would say with regret that the Court has ambled on and off for years, usually dragging in an audience when they put on a play that appealed to the Edwardian taste that passes for culture in the London press; or when it appealed directly to a rigidly defined social subsection, who would not support it when it changed its appeal to some other subsection. It does not – cannot – have a regular new audience because it has not dedicated itself to creating a radical new culture, one that will create a moral and practical consciousness appropriate to life in the last years of this century. (p. 124)

Those critics who feel that Bond is ungratefully biting the hand that fed him here should attend very carefully to the implications of the final sentence: it expresses succinctly that firm belief in the ethical function of theatre which is basic to his work.

There is an amusing irony in the fact that before *Saved* established Bond as a major writer, the only performance previously staged had been *The Pope's Wedding* which as decor had utilised the set of George Devine's production of *Happy Days*: Winnie's mound was inverted, a door cut in it and a 'funny sort of cone shape' resulted. The step from this first play to the tensile force of *Saved* was a big one. The Court, like the English theatre, was not ready for *Saved*. This goes beyond the matter of censorship. The *furore* which erupted entirely obscured any real consideration of either the play's theatrical merits or Bond's purpose in writing it. The play is a document, an exposé of an area of life that would be unfamiliar to the audience watching it. It asks the audience to relate their own middle-class values to those observed in the drama and ask why they are so different. What causes such brutality – both in the conduct of the gang and the behaviour in the home? What is the right – the just, the rational – attitude to take to it? These are the questions posed by the play and addressed squarely to a select and specific audience. The English Stage Society, encountering similar problems with the Lord Chamberlain's censorship office as had arisen over Osborne's homosexual drama *A Patriot For Me* the previous year, resorted to the same ruse: they offered the play as a private performance to club members only.

This initiated the struggle which had ultimately very little to do with the ethical debate Bond was proposing. The struggle marked the final stage in the Court's own fight against censorship and led to the abolishing of the Lord Chamberlain as censor of plays in 1968. This occurred only after he had objected to Bond's next play, *Early Morning* and the Court had again defied him – albeit for only one performance. Morally they had won: though they were taken to Court over *Saved* and found guilty (of not operating a *bona fide* members club) the small fine imposed on them made the Lord Chamberlain appear almost as much a fool as he did by objecting to *Early Morning in toto*. The whole ethical debate however, had significantly shifted from a social to an aesthetic basis. What was at issue was the freedom of the artist and for this the Royal Court was prepared to fight to the last. *Saved* and *Early Morning* gave them a principle for which to fight.

The extent to which the ground had shifted can be seen from the numerous apologia which insisted on playing down the vital issues of the plays. Choosing to ignore the force of the political satire in *Early Morning*, which exposes Victorian morality in presenting a murdurous and lesbian Queen Victoria finally consummating her life-style in a cannibalistic heaven, Martin Esslin insisted:

> Seldom in the history of human folly can there have been so much ado about so little! Whether Edward Bond's play is deemed good or bad, significant or insignificant, entertaining or boring, may be open to dispute. But one thing surely must be beyond dispute for anyone capable of giving it only a few minutes' clear logical thought: the play is *totally inoffensive*. (*Plays and Players* June 1968 p. 26)

This was matched by Charles Marowitz's review which combined a contempt for censorship with a patronising dismissal of the play:

> Bond's play throws up two separate issues which, in London, have tended to get confused. 1) Neither the police nor the Lord Chamberlain should prevent this play from reaching the public, and 2) if it did, the ultimate censorship, which would certainly annihilate it, is the resounding apathy it would inspire in most people unfortunate enough to be lured into its pseudo-pornographic orbit. (*Confessions of a Counterfeit Critic* p. 142)

Later Marowitz was to revise his opinion after directing the play himself and to recognise its savage satiric potential. In the hullabaloo which surrounded the first productions of *Saved* and *Early Morning* such considerations took second place to a quixotic fight against an outmoded censor. When a similar situation arose over the staging of *The Romans In Britain* in 1980 the director revealed himself prepared to face prison for his right to stage the work. One wonders whether he would have defended so avidly the political principles which the play upholds.

Such was the theatrical environment which Bond entered in the mid 'sixties and which his plays did much to change. His next work *Narrow Road To The Deep North*, taking its inspiration from the writings of the sixteenth century Japanese poet Matsu Basho and in presenting a conflict between Asian tyranny and European colonialism, was very different. It was written not for the Royal Court but for the Belgrade Theatre Coventry and reveals in some senses a pronounced reaction against that distortion of his political intentions which had characterized the critical reaction to his earlier plays there. Of *Narrow Road* he commented in 'the Lively Arts' on B.B.C. Radio 4 on March 26th 1969: 'I regard the play as critic fodder really . . . it's a very easy light little play. In a sense I wrote it so quickly just to prove that I could do it . . . because (the critics) just hadn't understood a word of the first performance of *Early Morning*.' The theme of the play – expressed through a straightforward narrative – is stated with a clarity that is sharply at odds with the paradoxes of *Saved* or the sustained anachronism of *Early Morning*. Not until 1971 did Bond return to the Court, to the scope and complexity of his earlier plays and to a more productive collaboration with Gaskill who had staged and championed both *Early Morning* and *Saved*. By this time censorship was a thing of the past and Bond – who had been able to reach the general public only with his fourth play – was now able to speak to them without restraints.

Before returning to the Court, Bond wrote two quite different pieces and for very different venues. In each case the production was conceived as a demonstration, a single performance of a play making a direct, hard-hitting point. On March 22nd 1970 *Black Mass* was performed at the Lyceum Theatre – Sir Henry Irving's old theatre, now converted to a Mecca dance hall – as a direct statement on the Sharpeville massacre in South Africa. This was agit prop theatre: a political statement with the force and savagery of a political cartoon. Bond himself played Christ, hanging from a crucifix in a South African church. A priest and Prime Minister, taking communion, are interrupted by a police chief who warns them of the native threat. As gunfire is heard off-stage they leave, Christ descends from the cross and poisons the communion wine. When the minister returns he drinks the wine and dies. Jesus is the only suspect. He is expelled and a riot cop ordered to take his place. As Michael Kustow commented in *The Listener*: 'It is a George Grosz picture come to life, it is ghastly, it is the only possible kind of artistic imagery through which to speak of such evil'. On April 11th 1971 Bond matched this with another propaganda piece *Passion*, written for the Campaign For Nuclear Disarmament and performed at Alexandra Park racecourse. The space demanded a larger-than-life cartoon style which perfectly suited Bond's essentially visual imagination. The Narrator tells a story involving on Old Woman, a Dead Soldier, a Queen, a Prime Minister and a Magician in which the Old Woman appeals to the Queen to have her dead son restored to her. The entrances of the Queen singing 'The Campdown Races' and the Prime Minister singing 'A Life on the Ocean Wave', both playing with a yo-yo, indicate the essential style of the piece which culminates in the arrival of Christ and Buddha who are also powerless to help. Buddha's comment on the Queen and the Prime Minister: 'You see, they are mad. They have no pity. They can't pity each other, so how could they ever listen to us?' recalls Arthur in *Early Morning* and anticipates the ultimate cry of Lear in Bond's next play. The moral centre of Bond's work remains the same; but he is able to change his dramatic style to match the different occasions and theatrical spaces for which he writes.

Bond's *Lear* certainly revealed that he had lost nothing of his bite. At last he was able to write and see his plays performed without the intervention of the censor. Undoubtedly *Lear* could not have been written prior to the demise of the Lord Chamberlain. The scenes of violence exceed anything in his previous plays; indeed the drama appears in some respects to be a study of violence, of the different forms it takes in military and civilian life. This is not the theme of the play, but the visual and physical force of the play's imagery is in danger of eclipsing the social and political argument. Here Bond, assisted by a wholly sympathetic director, Gaskill, presented his most sustained attack on political corruption, blindness and hypocrisy. This was a play, like Osborne's *A Patriot For Me*, which stretched to the full the potential of the Royal Court stage. In his Casebook, published in *Theatre Quarterly*, Gregory Dark explains the challenges this represented to the cast of 23 playing over eighty parts and recreating scenes in a wide variety of locations. But there is a lesson to be learnt from the Chichester revival of *A Patriot For Me* in 1983. Given the resources of a much larger, thrust stage, Ronald Eyre padded out the original with irrelevant crowd scenes and elaborate scene changes. As a result the play lost all its force and drive. Osborne knew what he was doing on the Royal Court stage and so did Bond. The belief that they were somehow constricted by the limitations of the theatre would occur only to someone unaware of the real strengths of the space. In *Lear* Bond was able to create a fast-moving epic which at the same time allowed him the precision of close-up which is intrinsic to the small theatre. When he came to write another sort of epic – for the Olivier stage of the National Theatre – his effects expanded and were able to unfold at a different pace.

Lear was followed by *The Sea*, a drama which marks the

end of what Bond sees as the first phase of his creative writing. He sees the opening up of a debate which begins with Scopey's determination to enter into the mind of the old recluse, Alen – an impossibility, as the title of the play, *The Pope's Wedding*, reminds us – and which ends with Evens's conversations with Willy and the aggressive Hollarcut at the end of *The Sea*. The connection between the violent events of *Lear* and the calmer acceptance of death in *The Sea* has a parallel with Shakespeare's development from *King Lear* to *The Tempest* and receives further dramatic treatment in Bond's next play *Bingo*. In *The Sea* Bond created a drama which in its wit and tenderness has most in common with the style of drama pioneered by the Court. The combination of historical perspective, social comment and psychological truth makes the play one of Bond's most successful and popular. It is the only one to have been televised in Britain, and the play elicited some of the most successful performances to date in his work. Coral Browne, who played the overbearing Mrs Rafi, the tyrant of a small sea-coast town in the first decade of the century, gave a performance which captured the wit and pathos of the character whilst allowing us to see beyond that to the writer's very different social and political perspective. As Martin Esslin said:

> Coral Browne plays that scene (the penultimate one) with superb control, the marble brow of haughty self-assurance which she carried before her in previous scenes, suddenly crumbles and falls away and underneath it are the pallid features of a cornered animal. Only the finest actress could manage the transition from polished high comedy to this depth of tragic intensity and insight. (*Plays and Players*, July 1973 p. 47)

Bond remarked, challengingly, 'I do consciously write

for people who behave on the stage. When I write a part for
Shakespeare, I do have in a certain sense the technique of
someone like Frankie Howerd in mind'. (T. Coult: *The
Plays of Edward Bond* p. 73) After this it is a shock to find
Sir John Gielgud playing the part of Shakespeare. He did
not play it originally: in the first production, at the
Northcott Theatre Exeter on 14th November 1973 Bob
Peck created the part. But when the play transferred to the
Royal Court it was recast. Bond has expressed his admira-
tion for Gielgud's acting:

> I greatly admired Gielgud's handling of language: his
> ability to make every word count, to judge the emphasis
> and meaning precisely. This is a result of great cunning
> and art. When you listen to Gielgud, at least in a text that
> stretches him, you hear the brain and not just the voice –
> and even if you don't always agree with the brain, it is at
> least a pleasure to listen to the brain: with many actors
> you only hear their voice, and that is very boring. (Letter
> to the author: 4.8.84.)

The majesty of Gielgud's celebrated vocal tones, however,
in some respects tended to romanticise and glamorise
Bond's portrait, giving the character a dignity at variance
with the playwright's harsher analysis of him. Such an
emphasis misled some of the critics, most notably Garry
O'Connor, into a condemnation of Bond's method:

> His progress as a playwright is from the direct, cold-
> blooded infanticide of *Saved* to the more refined literary
> assassination of *King Lear* (a mythological figure of
> English culture), and now, in *Bingo*, the more abstract
> assassination of Shakespeare's reputation (a writer who
> lived a blameless life, happened to be gifted with genius,

and probably believed in original sin) (*Plays and Players*, September 1974 p. 26)

Ironically O'Connor is absolutely right in emplying the word 'mythological' to describe the basis of Bond's examination of Shakespeare in this work: he wishes to look beyond the myth of the 'sweet swan of Avon' retiring to the bosom of his family at the end of his career and survey the compromises he made, as revealed by an examination of historical evidence and the economic realities of the age.

If Gielgud was a far cry from Frankie Howerd, Arthur Lowe, who played Ben Jonson in the Royal Court production, struck perfectly that note of self disgust mixed with an ironic perception of the world which is common to Bond's portrait of both artists and which Gielgud obscured. As Bond has said:

> If you go back to Frankie Howerd, the extraordinary thing was, one realized in a sense one was performing a dance with him. You weren't sitting there listening, he was reacting to you all the time. You knew what the climax was, but you worked together for it. (Coult p. 73)

This observation of a performance skill which is appropriate to popular theatre and which Brecht would have endorsed is characteristic of Bond who later, as a director, can be seen to encourage actors not to form too close an involvement with the life of the character they are presenting and to insist instead on an objectivity which arises from an awareness of the specific circumstances in which the figure is placed.

Bond has said that he conceived of *Bingo* and the two plays which followed as a trilogy in which he attempted to 'deal with society at three important stages of cultural development. The past often works as a myth on the present. It is like a burden on our back and from time to time we have to rearrange it so that it becomes comfortable and we can go on with our journey.' (Letter to Tony Coult, reprinted in Hay and Roberts: *Companion*, p. 74). *Bingo* examines the role of the artist at the beginning of the seventeenth century and his sense of guilty compromise in the land-enclosure movement. *The Fool* dramatises the life of John Clare, the farm labourer turned poet, who was unable to support the working class in the period of industrialisation at the beginning of the nineteenth century. *The Woman* explores the myth of Greek civilization and its relevance to our own history. None of these plays was directed by Gaskill; only one of them was first performed at the Royal Court. They mark Bond's break with the theatre which had been central to his work for over ten years, *The Woman* being his first production at the National Theatre and directed by Bond himself. Bond has returned only once to the Court since *The Fool* was staged there in 1975, and it proved to be one of his least successful productions.

Before mounting his production of *The Woman* at the Olivier theatre and in the same year his first play for the Royal Shakespeare Company: *The Bundle*, Bond was involved in two very different types of theatre. One is represented by the opera *We Come To The River* at Covent Garden and the adaptation of *The White Devil* at the Old Vic; in the same year – 1976 – he created two other pieces of agit-prop theatre, developing the techniques first explored in *Black Mass* and *Passion* six years earlier. In response to a request from Gay Sweatshop he created a political parable, *Stone*. This is a short play in seven scenes, strongly recalling Brecht's 'Lehrstücke': the 'teaching pieces' such as *The Measures Taken* and *The Exception and the Rule*. *Stone* more fully resembles the latter, telling an amusingly ironic story of a young man undertaking a journey full of hope with the seven gold talents his thrifty parents have given him and losing them through his various encounters with representatives of exploitation. In an interview with *Gay News* Bond explained the purpose of his drama which makes no direct reference to homosexualty by saying: 'There must be those situations where oppression is made to identify itself. You must tread on its toes and make it declare itself. (*Gay News* 17-30 June 1976.) Bond here refuses to deal with any specific type of oppression particular to the homosexual, preferring instead to teach a wider economic and political lesson. The play, performed at the Institute of Contemporary Arts, was clearly designed for a sophisticated middle class audience. It is very different from the style of play which characterised the work of Gay Sweatshop at the time, a group torn between the social awareness of writers such as Noel Grieg and Drew Griffiths on the one hand and the aggressive separatism of the women who scorned any political commitment as part of male oppression on the other. In some senses Bond's play is as much a response to the political confusion of gay minorities as a comment on their enemies.

A–A–America, a double bill of two short plays, *Grandma Faust* and *The Swing* written for Inter-Action's Almost Free Theatre in the same year, is very different. The plays were commissioned as part of the American Connection season (a celebration of the two hundredth anniversary of the signing of the Declaration of Independence) and inspired in Bond his most direct political onslaught to date. The first play – a burlesque – shows the Devil (Grandma Faust) attempting through a hillbilly caricature of Uncle Sam to capture the soul of a black, Paul. This satire on American values prepares us thematically for the second play. In style, however, *The Swing* – described as 'a

documentary' is Bond's most savage play. We are told by
Paul of how in Kentucky in 1911 a black man was executed
for murder. Tied to a stake on the stage of the local theatre
he was shot by the patrons who paid a fixed price for every
bullet they were then allowed to shoot. The events of *The
Swing* lead us to believe that Paul will be accused of rape
and forced to be shot; in fact Fred, his sympathetic white
friend, is selected as the victim. We are taken off guard and
then made to be accomplices as the theatre, an old
vaudeville house which is being converted into a store,
previously the setting for the story, becomes the stage on
which Fred is brutally executed in front of us. Here Bond
employs the atmosphere of a small club theatre to disturb
his audience by confronting them with extreme violence in
a realistic and intimate way. As Tony Coult, reviewing the
performance at the Almost Free commented:

> The richness and subtlety of the writing and the match-
> ing power of the dramatic structure unite to create a play
> that works like a sort of moral vaccine. By infecting the
> audience with some responsibility for the events, and
> confronting it with its own dark potential, the play seeks
> to generate antibodies against other more immediate
> plagues. (*Plays and Players* February 1977 p. 37)

On August 10th 1978, Bond produced his first play at the
National Theatre. This was *The Woman*, a large epic play
with a cast of over fifty, retelling the story of the fall of Troy
and its aftermath. The play was mounted on the largest of
the three stages at the National: the Olivier, and deliberate-
ly exploited to the full its scope and architectural links with
the theatre of classical Greece. Of this stage Bond wrote:

> It has resources of space, time, skill and technology that

41

we can use to strengthen our work and relate it more closely to our age. We use advanced technology to travel to our jobs and to bake bread, and there must also be times when we use it to create those images of ourselves which are essential to culture and human nature. The stone age artist used the advanced technology of his time, and we must use ours. We must not merely occupy the fringe but the centre. (*Us, Our Drama and the National Theatre. Plays and Players.* October 1978 p. 8)

Bond likened the Olivier stage to a public square, the meeting of several roads, a playing field or a factory floor, insisting that 'we need to set our scenes in public places, where history is formed, classes clash and whole societies move.' For Bond such a theatre is ideal; whilst it does not pretend to accommodate the whole state as the Greek theatre did, or a cross section of society like the Elizabethan playhouse, it represents the largest meeting place for the audience Bond wishes to reach and offers the richest resources.

Directors at the National have been slow to exploit the space to its full. Not since Peter Hall's early production of Marlowe's *Tamburlaine* has the full dynamic force of the thrust stage been utilised. When Bond examined the theatre he found a tall metal fire wall painted black and masked by black drapes at the very back. He and the designer, Hayden Griffin opened the stage up to this wall. The paint was stripped off and the wall became part of the design concept, representing the walls of Troy in Part One and, differently lit, the sea and sky of Part Two. No scenery was used and the actors, as in the classical Greek theatre, dominated the stage. This effect of magnification at first exposed the weakness of the company who were 'acting emotions, hugging feelings to themselves' so that they were in effect 'private performers on a public stage.' In working with them to correct this, Bond explored new techniques in order to shift the actors' emphasis from the personal to the social. Insisting that his play describe 'situations, not characters' Bond trained the actors in the crowd scenes to present the significant shifts of the action – in the scene (Part One, scene 12) when they capture the statue, for example – through bold, clear, unified gestures. He defended this against the critics who felt the crowd lacked individuality by insisting on the need to focus on the social and political event, a feature of epic theatre which applies equally to the individual actor:

> Telling such a story, describing history, needs a new sort of acting. Put roughly and briefly it is this. A concept, an interpretation (of the situation, not the character) must be applied to an emotion, and it is this concept or interpretation or idea that is acted. This relates the character to the social event so that he becomes its story teller. When this is done emotions are transferred to the surface. Instead of being hidden in the heart or the gut (or other corners of the bourgeois soul) they go to the hands, feet, face, head and become living creative energy. Then the actor is freed to interpret the situation. (*op. cit.* p. 9)

Earlier the same year – the 13th of January – Bond worked for the first time with the other major subsidised theatrical company in Britain, the Royal Shakespeare Company. *The Bundle*, in which he returned to the subject of *Narrow Road To The Deep North*, was performed at the Warehouse, the smaller, more intimate space used by the company in London. Bond had been working on *The Woman* for several years since its original conception; *The Bundle*, though performed earlier, is a later work, marking the first of his 'answer plays', and thus a new phase in his development. In this piece – and in all the plays since – he has been concerned to find answers to the problems he had previously exposed. His aim – which was to crystallise more precisely a little later – has been to 'dramatise the analysis': to encourage the audience to use the plays as material with which they might reconstruct their own lives, replacing outmoded and inefficient ethics with a more practical and rational attitude.

Bond has always been first and foremost a teacher. It is therefore not surprising to see him involving himself with students more in the last few years. In May 1977 he accepted an Honorary Doctorate at Yale University and in October of the same year took up a two-year Northern Arts Literary Fellowship in the Universities of Newcastle and Durham. From October 1982 to March 1983 he was Resident Theatre Writer at the University of Essex. In October and November 1983 he acted as Visiting Professor at the University of Palermo, Sicily. Most recently when asked by a group of my ex-students – from the University of Birmingham – who had formed a theatre group with the aim of expanding socialist theatre in the Midlands, he wrote a play for them and himself assisted with the direction. His work as a teacher is intimately bound up with his life as a creative writer, though the experience of working with students has not always been easy. His stay at Essex proved unsatisfactory, though Bond has published a number of extracts from the play, he created there: *After The Assassinations*. By contrast, after his work at Newcastle he produced one of his most complex and assured plays to date: *The Worlds*.

This play was first performed by Newcastle University Theatre Society at the Newcastle Playhouse on the 8th March 1979 and in London by the Activists Youth Theatre

Club at the Royal Court Theatre Upstairs on 21st November. The play was conceived for and performed at first by young people, unprofessional actors. This in no way compromised Bond, who not only created a number of powerful confrontations in the drama, between big business management, militant strikers and terrorists, but expanded the issues of the work in the *Activists Papers*, an exploration of the political problems treated in the play and the theatrical techniques employed to dramatise them. Since young amateur actors are free from the preconceptions and sophisticated approach of professionals, Bond was able to avoid the clichés of conventional acting technique and present the argument of his play clearly and directly. The in-built alienation effect of young actors representing older characters assisted this and made it possible to concentrate on the debate rather than the performance.

The problems of professional stagings of Bond's work were never more in evidence than in the production of his next play *Restoration*, the latest work of his to be performed at the Royal Court. It was premiered there on 21st July 1981 with Simon Callow playing the villainous and witty Lord Are in a pastiche of eighteenth century drama which is used as a social criticism both of the period and of our own. Callow himself has explained in his book *Being An Actor* that he was very dissatisfied with his performance. Though admiring the play immensely, he confesses to being at a loss in understanding the character or how to play him, and that Bond's direction was unhelpful. His own admission that he sought a way of understanding the character by reference to animal characteristics reveals an alien approach to Bond's theatre which requires the performer to see his role in the context of the society around him and not in relation to psychological formulae or codes of physical stage behaviour. Bond is sceptical of the tricks on which professional actors rely to persuade themselves they are coming to terms with the character: he once cited to me the example of Olivier who proudly announced that he was getting nearer to understanding the part he was playing since he had 'got the character's hat.' Bond is suspicious of acquired and polished theatrical technique as well as the indulgence in emotional acting which is seen at its most extreme in the American Method school. He has immense admiration for an actress such as Yvonne Bryceland, who from her years in South Africa has an intimate knowledge of political oppression and who brings an awareness of other issues than the emotional to the parts she plays. She created the role of Hecuba in *The Woman* and that of Marthe in *Summer* when the play was premiered on the Cottesloe stage of the National Theatre on 27th January 1982.

Bond will no doubt continue to explore a wide variety of theatrical possibilities both in terms of venues and techniques. In 1983 he completed another full-length epic play for the National Theatre: *Human Cannon* with a huge cast and a rich variety of scenes exploring the ethics of revolution during the Spanish Civil War. His collaboration with Henze – developed in the writing of a scenario for a ballet *Orpheus* performed by the Stuttgart Ballet Company in 1979 – more recently resulted in another music theatre piece *The Cat* performed (under the title of *The English Cat*) by the Stuttgart Staatsoper in 1983.

Meanwhile Bond has been busy with a number of very different shorter works. His interest in creating pieces for young actors resulted in *Derek*, a cunning political parable in which a brilliant working class boy is forced to sell his brain to a wealthy industrialist's son who has a mental age of ten. This was performed at the Royal Shakespeare

Company's Youth Festival in 1982. In 1983 Bond wrote another piece for the R.S.C. – *Red, Black and Ignorant* – in which a black charred Monster tells of the nuclear holocaust and informs the audience that he and two others will 'act scenes from the life I did not live.' This clever theatrical device allows Bond to speak of the present and the future simultaneously to warn of the economic and cultural reasons which are leading to an escalation of the arms race. This was followed earlier in 1984 by the play commissioned by the Midlands' ex-student group Bread and Circuses: *The Tin Can People* which with a cool Shavian logic examines 'as far as thought can reach' – the consequences of nuclear war. This is the second of three plays Bond has conceived as a trilogy on this subject. Having looked at significant periods and movements in our history, Bond – the political writer most acutely concerned with our present – has now begun more fully to explore what our future could hold in store.

3
Diabolonian Ethics, Techniques of Subversion

> . . . I find that my work is more radical than I had thought. I
> began writing simply as a criticism of certain things I saw
> around me, and in praise of certain other things. I wanted to
> understand and so I had to analyze. I didn't at that time
> understand the implications this would have on my theatrical
> technique.
> Notebook on *Restoration*

'Saved'

Saved was the play which brought Bond to the attention of
the theatre-going public in 1965. Though it lacks the satiric
onslaught of *Early Morning* – which was banned *in toto* by
the Lord Chamberlain – and it does not advocate the cause
of revolution as his later plays have done, it is in some
respects an even more disturbing and challenging drama.
This is because of the uncompromising presentation of the
action through a sharply realistic style which exposes the
more acutely the paradox at the centre of the play. We are

forced to see the harsh details of the world both through the eyes of the protagonist, Len, and through those of Bond. We are presented with an accurate and minutely detailed picture of life which functions simultaneously as a savage criticism of the social and political composition of contemporary Britain. In twenty years the play has lost nothing of its immediacy; indeed growing unemployment and a shift towards more reactionary Victorian values on the part of the government have increased the truth of its criticism of social and political truths. The play forces us to see working-class people, as Len does 'at their worst and most hopeless', and yet refuses to allow us any easy or convenient moral indignation through which to vent the feelings of sympathy and anger which it provokes.

It is a long play, unfolding in thirteen independent yet inter-connected scenes a bleak prospect of contemporary life. Set in South London, it alternates between a working-class home, a prison, a cafe and a park. Beginning with an amusing scene of interrupted love-making and ending with a grim scene of social stalemate set in the same room, it portrays cruelty, violence and murder which are the more credible as they are intimately related to their recognisable, everyday setting. Bond was employing a realistic dramatic technique, familiar from the work of previous Royal Court authors, but he refines this to give his social and political satire added force. This is evident in the first scene in which Pam has picked up Len and brought him home. Their conversation has the terseness of Pinter's dialogue, but there is absolutely no sub-text here. Indeed, the barrenness of their exchanges is a comment on the emptiness of their culture, itself a reflection of the deprivation which is characteristic of their social situation:

LEN.   This ain' the bedroom.

PAM. Bed ain' made.

LEN. Oo's bothered?

PAM. It's awful. 'Ere's nice.

LEN. Suit yourself. Yer don't mind if I take me shoes off? (*He kicks them off*). No one 'ome?

PAM. No.

LEN. Live on yer tod?

PAM. No.

LEN. O.

(*Plays: One* p. 21.)

The scene is both an accurate realistic portrayal of this situation and a very funny introduction to the drama.

Bond's purpose however is not to comment on the *mores* of these working class figures – as Pinter does in *The Homecoming* or Orton in *Entertaining Mr Sloane* – but to present a life-style which is conditioned entirely by social circumstances. Pam and Len have a great deal of fun at the expense of Harry, Pam's father who interrupts them whilst preparing to leave for work. The salacious *double-entendres* which Len shouts as he is offering Pam a sweet are funny, but a firm comment on the impoverishment of his language and imagination. The social context of the scene is brought into clearer focus when we realise that Harry is about to work a night-shift. Hence he disturbs what little privacy the two lovers have. As we shall see, these issues – at first kept in the background, as Bond's initial aim is to amuse and grip his audience – assume a greater focus as the play develops and we are made to see the correlation between the cramped conditions of the home, the domestic tension this breeds, and the violence which is its inevitable expression both inside and outside the house.

When a group of my students performed *Saved* in the

Allardyce Nicoll Studio of the Birmingham Department of
Drama and Theatre Arts Bond sent them a '*Short Note of
Violence and Culture*' which included this statement:

> I know, of course, that an unhappy home might make
> one person a criminal and another a saint – people
> always respond individually. But it follows that contact
> with a saint might make someone else into a criminal.
> There is no way out of these pessimistic reflections
> unless we understand that, as a whole, a community
> takes on the characteristic of its culture – that set of ideas
> and culture by which the society functions. These ideas
> and customs are largely laid down by the owners and
> rulers of society. It is the individual's response to these
> ideas and customs that sets the character of a society. We
> are not creatures of instinct but of culture.

The paradox which characterises the opening of this
comment is explained by the conclusion. Society unjustly
deprives many of its members – specifically and literally the
working people – in that they are denied economic and
social conditions productive of a healthy culture. The
resultant violence, bred of ignorance and frustration, is
therefore the fault as much of society as of the individual.
Bond's concept of culture – as we see from his other works –
is not of some privileged acquisition, reserved for a select
few, the icing on the cake, but rather the foundation on
which society is built. A society lacking culture is a society
lacking reason. Bond's firm belief in the possibility of
creating a new and sane culture – one based on Marxist
criteria and not on antiquated concepts of privilege – is the
basis of his own continued and growing optimism.

It is important to see this so as not to fall into the trap of
finding *Saved* a pessimistic play. Bond sees it as 'almost

irresponsibly optimistic' precisely because he sees beyond the catalogue of violent events the play presents. These are grim indeed but Bond both examines why they occur and how they can be prevented. The scene which provoked the maximum controversy when the play was first performed and which is still profoundly disturbing is that which culminates in the murder of Pam's child. What makes the scene so theatrically effective is the psychological truth of the presentation gained through a telling observation of the attitudes of the boys: every detail is grounded in observation of social and economic fact. Pam's treatment of the baby emphasises its status as an object, moreover as an inconvenient object which has been ignored throughout scene four and has now been drugged with aspirin. It is not enough however, to dismiss Pam's attitude as occasioned by apathy and viciousness; we are forced to evaluate the influence of her home life and beyond that, the economic situation which has conditioned this.

The attitude of the boys matches hers, but has an added element of macho bravado which makes it even more appalling. Barry's distortion of the nursery rhyme:

Rock a bye baby on a tree top
When the wind blows the cradle will rock
When the bough breaks the cradle will fall
And down will come baby cradle and tree
    an' bash its little brains out an' dad'll scoop
    'em up and use 'em for bait'

is guaranteed to provoke laughter; it is he who also initiates the obscene joking with the balloon which follows. Bond is precisely pin-pointing the culture of these boys here. It is an empty and vicious one but the dramatist's condemnation reaches beyond individual psychology to wider social

implications. Theirs is a culture based on contempt for life; hence the attitude to sex as obscene, the occasion for smutty jokes and physical assaults on one another. In its combination of boasting and contempt for women Mike's insistence on the availability of casual sex in the local church and late-night laundries is a further comment on this culture. The escalating violence is entirely comprehensible in terms of bravado and consideration of the child as a dirty sub-human creature with no feelings whose punishment 'is therefore justified'. There is no sadism in the attitude of the boys in this scene; their cruelty is cold, unfeeling. It is precisely because it is inexplicable in terms of straightfor-ward emotional psychology that we are forced to consider the deeper psychological motivation which relates their action to the social and economic situation. It is for this reason that Bond's realism is essentially philosophical and political.

It is misleading to pay exclusive attention to the killing of the baby in evaluating the political purpose of Bond in this play. No less telling is the scene of domestic violence which erupts after the sexual encounter between Mary and Len. Harry, who has not spoken to his wife as long as Pam can remember, is goaded into response by Mary's advances to Len and she returns his verbal abuse with physical assault. Bond's observation of this silent battle of wills between husband and wife is one of the most accurate and emotive features of the play. It precisely defines an all-too-familiar working-class situation where incompatibility develops into hatred through an inability to communicate. The refusal to speak to one another is the ultimate expression of the barrenness of this culture: a more articulate couple might bicker, abuse one another verbally: Harry and Mary have no tools to help them; the fault is seen to be both theirs and society's. When the violence does erupt – in Mary's throwing of the bread on the floor and her hitting Harry over the head with the teapot – it is seen to be childish, pathetic. They have been reduced to animals by their way of life: Mary's dull household routine and Harry's enervating night work are inescapable realities of their economic situation, emphasised the more fully by Pamela's attitude to Len, which shows every sign of repeating the pattern established by her parents. Bond sees this as a consequence of a capitalist society which has a vested interest in exploiting the labour force and is quite unconcerned with a policy of wider cultural advancement. The solution – as he has come to see – requires a more radical re-ordering of society, though even in this play he lays down bases for a positive way forward. Len's attitude is fundamentally different from Pam's, from the other boy's and even from Harry's – who, though he reaches a new depth of understanding with Len, cannot stop nurturing his hatred for Mary. Len is the first of Bond's heroes: he learns a great deal in the play and this gives him a tenacity which he refuses to abandon. At the centre of the final scene of social stalemate he continues doggedly to mend the chair Harry broke in the row with Mary. One has only to compare Len with Beattie Bryan in Arnold Wesker's *Roots* to be fully aware of Bond's rejection of a political conversion founded essentially on personal issues and expressing itself in an attempt to convert her family to her newly acquired taste for classical music. For Bond such an acceptance of the cultural values of another class serves merely to cover over the wound; more radical surgery is needed to cure the political disease.

The precise nature of Bond's approach in *Saved* is very similar to that employed by Shaw for parallel social and economic criticism in *Mrs Warren's Profession*. Shaw declared in the Preface to this play that he wrote the drama not as an indictment of moral depravity on the part of either prostitutes or their clients, but as an exposé of the monstrous economic system which made it expedient for women to prostitute themselves rather than undertake a worse-paid, more physically arduous job. In a no less impassioned Preface Bond makes it clear that in *Saved* he is pointing a critical finger not so much at the obscenity of the gang's violence as at the iniquitous social and economic situation which gives rise to it. The basic techniques of both dramatists is the use of paradox. They both play down their condemnation of what is conventionally considered to be the ultimate in amoral behaviour so as to focus on conduct they consider to be worse. Shaw employed this strategy in many of his plays. In the Preface to *The Devil's Disciple* he explains his method in an essay entitled *On Diabolonian Ethics*: his technique is similar to that of William Blake in that he intends to confound conventional morality by exposing its hypocrisy and arguing for a more rational approach to society. In the programme for *Saved* Bond included the Blake quote: 'Better strangle an infant in its cradle than nurse unacted desires' and he went on to expand the implications of this in his Preface to the play:

> Clearly the stoning to death of a baby in a London park is a typical English understatement. Compared to the 'strategic' bombing of German towns it is a negligible atrocity, compared to the cultural and emotional deprivation of most of our children its consequences are insignificant. (*Plays: One*, pp. 310-11)

This is meant to be provocative. Those who are morally indignant at the killing of a child are not at first likely to connect this with the defense strategies or economic policies of the government. But Bond intends us to do so.

When we recognise that public violence is a direct result of political aggression and social inequality we can stop making glib moralistic pronouncements on such conduct. As he said in his note to my students:

> Unfortunately since we live in a small world we have to think not of national society but rather of a world society. It then becomes clear that our species is threatened not by social criminals but by political ones: those who threaten us with the ultimate crime of nuclear holocaust. With the class of leaders we have we must expect to find violence on the streets. This is not because people are barbarous – but because our society is.

It is clear that Bond's drama is subversive of conventional religious and ethical values. He insists in the Preface to *Saved* that our children are morally bewildered because all the morality they are taught is grounded in religion. This religion has nothing to do with their parents' personal lives, or our economic, industrial and political life, and is contrary to the science and rationalism they are taught at other times. For them religion discredits the morality it is meant to support'. He concludes that we must teach 'moral scepticism and analysis, and not faith'. (*Plays: One*, pp. 311-2). This is precisely what *Saved* is designed to encourage: through its savage central paradox – the reality of a monstrous society responsible for the ugly violence we witness – he has found a spectacularly effective technique of provoking his audience both emotionally and, beyond that, intellectually.

Apart from the moral indignation of the Lord Chamberlain who insisted on cuts which would have made a performance of the play impossible, the reaction of another contemporary critic, the writer Pamela Handsford Johnson, is worth citing at this point. In 1967 Johnson published *On Iniquity*, an examination of the motives of Myra Hindley and Ian Brady, the moors murderers. In this study she reaches the conclusion that they were both corrupted by the pornography they read, and thus anything which might be classified as likely to deprave or corrupt should be banned – not however to all, but to those whose defective education might make them susceptible to its influence. The paternalistic elitism of this approach illustrates the sort of morality Bond despises, and it is no surprise to find Johnson listing *Saved* among precisely those works that are likely to corrupt. She says:

> I do not speak of this play lightly. I have read and re-read it with the greatest care, and remain of the opinion that the scene to which I refer (scene 6) is, despite, its verbal skill, unfit for public representation. Either it sickens, or it conduces to the wrong kind of excitation. it is not conducive to social thinking, since it contains no shock of new knowledge (*On Iniquity*, p. 49).

It is significant that she had read the play and not seen it, and she failed wholly to grasp – or to accept – the implications of Bond's 'social thinking' in the work. The title of her book is perfectly expressive of her moral approach: precisely the opposite of Bond's. She believes in moral definitions of good and bad quite unrelated to social and political conditions. For her the boys in *Saved* along with Hindley and Brady are wicked: 'iniquitous', to employ her epithet. She upholds the conservative ethical values which are the corollary of her privileged social position. She expresses the desire to put an end to what she terms 'liberal' thinking which seeks to explain crime by reference to environment; rather she holds the belief that people are born good or bad, or that at least their conduct is entirely their own responsibility. It is a recognisable attitude and one wholly at variance with Bond's whose moral stand is no less clear, but whose radical approach to ethics is dependent on a wider social and political perspective. In the *Short Note On Violence and Culture* he states this firmly:

> In human beings the idea always takes precedent over instinct. This is a revolutionary concept because it completely changes the way in which we think of both human beings and their societies. It means that human beings act not in accordance with the emotions they bring into the world but in accordance with the ideas they are taught and acquire while they are in it. We think of emotions as motivating actions but really emotions spring from and are directed by ideas. This means that humanity is made by human beings – or rather by being human – and that ultimately when human beings are inhuman it is their interpretation of themselves and their society that is at fault. This does not mean that emotions have no importance but that they function in accordance with ideas. People become Nazis, for example, not because they have a particularly aggressive and ugly character but because their character is formed by certain ideas. These ideas then licence their emotions.

After *Saved* Bond determined to explore new theatrical techniques. Having written in a style familiar to Royal Court audiences and having, through this style, issued a more urgent political challenge, he felt the need to explore fresh dramatic forms. *Early Morning* is a radical departure from the downbeat realism of *Saved*, whilst *Narrow Road To The Deep North* saw the employment of incidents and techniques from Eastern theatre. Both *Lear* and *Bingo* employ a more subversive strategy: they respectively take a familiar Shakespearean play and details of Shakespeare's biography which they turn on their head, reaching conclusions which are at the furthest remove from received opinion and conventional interpretation. A tragedy concerned with the ethics of power is translated into a modern political morality play, and the traditional picture of the Bard retiring in peaceful fulfilment to his Stratford home is converted to a bleak examination of a failed artist's suicide. Shakespeare has exercised a large influence on Bond – who, like Shaw, has a love-hate relationship with his work. Bond, however, is not employing Shakespearean dramatic form in his re-write; *Lear* is the first exercise in his own brand of epic theatre. *The Sea*, *Bingo* and *The Fool* are also highly original in construction. *We Come To The River* marked a new departure: Bond was both constrained and inspired by the challenge of creating the libretto for an opera. It is after this work that he was to turn to other clearly definable examples of bourgeois theatrical form and by utilizing specific features expected by the audience, employ the dramatic medium for his own ends as a political writer. In so doing he is not deconstructing the idiom in which he is working: rather – as with *Saved* and *We Come To The River* – he is carrying to its ultimate conclusion the social and political potential inherent in the work of writers as diverse as Euripides, Farquhar and Ibsen.

'The Woman'

The first of these plays is *The Woman*, like the opera, written in response to the challenge of a new theatrical environment: the Olivier stage at the National Theatre. Bond responded to the aspects of the space which recall the

Greek amphitheatre and produced a play which in setting, scope and subject matter is strongly indebted to the drama of fifth century B.C. Athens. Between his initial conception of the play as *The Trojan Woman* early in 1974, and his completion of it (just over three years later) he spent two holidays in Malta where he soaked himself in the Mediterranean sun and re-read all the Greek tragedies. The result is a play owing a great deal to Euripides, both in respect of dramatic form and the subject matter taken from *The Trojan Woman*, but which also draws on other Greek plays such as Sophocles's *Oedipus* and *Antigone*. The scope of the drama is on the scale of *We Come To The River*. It has a large cast and narrates issues centering on two events: the fall of Troy and the arrival of the Greeks on a small Mediterranean island twelve years later. The play is in two very different parts, the first culminating in the tragic events consequent on the sack of Troy, the second leading to the liberation of the islanders from the Greeks as a result of the combined efforts and heroic action of Hecuba and the Dark Man. Hecuba is the central figure, active in both parts of the drama, moving from haughty contempt to despair in the first and from resignation to political action in the second. It is a progress which is familiar in Bond's drama. She has many affinities with Lear. Her attempt to blind herself after Troy has been taken has a parallel with the treatment he receives at the hands of his political enemies. It is also an echo of the climactic act of Sophocles's *Oedipus Rex*.

But like Oedipus – and like Bond's dramatic hero, Wang in *The Bundle* – Hecuba has more to learn. The process of her ethical and political awakening occupies the second act which is as different in style and subject matter from the first as is Sophocles's *Oedipus at Colonus* from the preceding tragedy. The significance of Ismene – a character taken from *Antigone*, the second of the Theban plays – alerts us to the importance of the entire trilogy in the overall structure of *The Woman*. In Sophocles's Theban dramas and in Aeschylus's *Orestaeia* the final note is one of hope. Oedipus learns wisdom, whilst at the conclusion of *The Eumenides* vengeance is converted to pity. In the latter Aeschylus is defending the political *status quo* through the decision of the Athenian court to temper justice with mercy. Bond's political aim is different. But it is significant that his own conclusion builds on the structure established by both these trilogies, the one dramatising enlightenment, the other attempting to put a stop to an inexorable concatenation of violent events.

That Bond wishes first to establish a recognisable dramatic context for the events of his play and, having drawn his bourgeois audience into this framework, then utilise it to teach fresh truths is borne out by the precisely similar technique he employs in a short poem published with the script of *The Woman*. This is entitled *Pompei* and begins with a description of everyday life in the city:

> People who lived on the slope
> Went to market each day
> Met on street corners
> Saw death in the arena
> And passed by sluices that carried water to wash
>   out the blood.

The jarring of this final line makes us suddenly aware of the complacent attitude to slaughter and torture, but this is a description of the past: of cruelty which no longer exists. The first verse continues:

> Took pains to bring up their children

61

Edward Bond

Brought horses and saved against age
While over the city the mountain smoked.

There follows a verse in which the violence and dangers hinted at in the first stanza are distanced by a liberal historical perspective:

It's said that in those days of imperial violence
Men lived in a dream
Learned how to live with danger
And energy gave way to frantic fever

This process, Bond is well aware, can easily set in whilst watching a historical play, the events of which no longer really touch us. That is why the political dramatist must make the audience aware of the relevance of the events they are witnessing to their own lives and force them to consider the implications more fully. In the poem this is effected by the shock of the sudden final line: 'How far is the missile site from your house?'

In the play the call to action also comes at the end, but throughout the audience is jolted by details which underline the contemporary relevance of the events staged. Bond's play centres on the power of a stolen statue. At the beginning of the play this has been taken to Troy; it replaces the abduction of Helen. We are on the eve of the fall of the city but the seige has continued for five years, not ten. Priam is dead, but he was not killed by Pyrrus and there is no mention of the Wooden Horse. The basic situation is the same as it is in Euripides's drama, but the details have been changed to make the modern parallel clearer. This emerges in the second part of the first scene when Greek leaders witness what is going on in Troy. This is seen entirely through the eyes of their leader, Heros, and, moreover, is acted out by the Greeks themselves: Nestor plays Hecuba, Thersites Cassandra and Ajax the Son. 'The scene', Bond informs us 'is to be imagined as occurring in Heros's head.' It presents a picture of Hecuba as a harridan refusing to listen to the advice of her family, notably over the matter of the statue:

> CASSANDRA. Give the statue to the Greeks. Without father to guide us –
> HECUBA. Trust the Greeks? No, I'll never do that. What would the Greeks have to lose once they'd got it? We must hold on to it – that's the only way to save our lives. (*The Woman* p. 17)

Here is the all-too-familiar cant of politicians supporting the arms race. It comes here with the full shock of awareness contained in the final line of *Pompei*: Hecuba's attitude calls attention to the same subject; hers is effectively a reactionary stand on disarmament. But this stand is the product of Heros's mistrust and fear of the Trojans; Hecuba is not like this at all, as we can see when we meet her. She readily falls in with Ismene's plan: to remain as a hostage in the city as a guarantee that once they have been given the statue the Greeks will go. The intuitive common sense of the women is in marked contrast to the conduct of the male leaders who refuse to act in this rational way. Hecuba's son has her imprisoned and himself fulfills the worst suspicions the Greeks had of the Trojans. He precipitates a bloody conflict which results in his own assassination, the destruction of the city, the murder of Astyanax and the enslavement of the women.

The 'Catch 22' situation exposed at the beginning of the play is seen to be entirely of the men's making. It serves to highlight the contemporary relevance of the drama but is not confined to the issue of disarmament. Bond is well aware that the real problem we are facing is the threat to the continuation of the species. Such a possibility is at the forefront in his mind and the destruction of an entire city and people is a pointed reminder of this. But the image of the statue serves to focus political issues of a different nature in the second act. By this point there are a number of survivors of the holocaust, living peacefully on an island. Hecuba's description of the waterspout that threatened to destroy them, but in fact separated them from their Greek oppressors, is another potent image of the danger from which they have escaped. But their peace is shattered by the arrival of Heros looking for them and the statue. Now his reason for taking the statue is to bolster his prestige in the new city he has established, but his chance of obtaining it is far more remote, as Hecuba informs him it has been lost at sea. The image of him fishing the seas to find it powerfully emphasises the folly of the politician desperately attempting to make his power secure, a course of action deflated by the attitude of Nestor who has little sympathy for Heros's insistence on punishing the soldier who has mistakenly allowed him through the lines:

> HEROS (to NESTOR). You think I'm unreasonable. This place is almost part of the sea. We *feel* it. All except you. Would you rush into a temple and yoo-hoo? I risk the welfare of Athens being here. It's our duty to take absolute care. We owe it to Athens. Yoo-Hooo! (*Distant roll of thunder*) It's a matter of military discipline. (Flatly). Now thunder.
>
> NESTOR. I'm surprised I'm not accused of farting. (*op. cit.* p.94)

The escalating madness of the ruler committed to maintaining an unjust society – familiar in Bond's work from *Early Morning* and *Lear* as well as *We Come To The River* –

culminates in Heros's acceptance of Hecuba's challenge to a race against the Dark Man. Though the latter is crippled he wins and Heros is killed. The Dark Man and Hecuba could be accused of cheating, but Bond argues that it is the duty of the political revolutionary to bide his time and strike down his oppressor when he is thoroughly trapped in the folly of his own desperate situation.

By the end of the play Bond has taken his audience a great deal further than they may well have anticipated in the opening scene of Act 1 with its action firmly grounded in the events of the Trojan war. In so doing he has fulfilled the duty of the Marxist writer. This is pithily explained in a further appendix to the drama: *Another Story*. Here he expresses in a brief narrative the point emphasised by Gramsci that we cannot come to terms with the future unless we understand the past. This story tells of a man, who, when lost, asked for directions from a woman and followed them. But he never reached his destination and, many years later, seeing the woman again, he asked why she had misled him. She apologised, assured him the directions had been right and that he must have misinformed her of his precise whereabouts. Bond's conclusion is:

> No one should set out on a journey till they know where they are starting. Indeed you may not know – perhaps never know – your destination: but you must know where you start. How else can you do anything or go anywhere? It follows that hope is not faith in the future but knowledge of the past. This hope is not an idle fiction but the surest of facts. It is a promise kept even before it is made. (*The Woman* p. 116)

This explains his interest not merely in the story of the Trojan war but also in the drama of Greek society in the fifth century B.C. 'I wanted', he has said, 'to go back and re-examine that world and how moral and rational it was, and whether or not it could be a valid example for a society like ours. I came to the conclusion that it wasn't'. (Unpublished interview with Tony Coult, August 1978. *H&RP.* p. 239) That society, however, was to provide him with a parallel with our own in another way.

The Trojan Women gave him – in Euripides's criticism of his own society – both the example of political expediency and military cruelty, and a dramatic model to use as the starting point of his own play. Euripides, the last of the three great Athenian tragic dramatists, has particular affinities with Bond. Lacking the clear-cut reactionary ethics of Aeschylus or the emphasis on individuals caught in a tragic pattern of fate which characterises the plays of Sophocles, he is a more satiric dramatist, critical of the conduct – social and political – of his contemporaries. *The Trojan Women* was inspired by his sense of outrage at a specific historical event: the savage attack on the defenceless island of Melos in 416 by the Greek forces led by Alcibiades. His play is in no sense an Aristotelian work, designed to lead the audience through a careful unity of action to identification with the central character and thus, through awareness of the reversal of his fortunes and recognition of this, effecting a purgation of the emotions of pity and terror. *The Trojan Women* is in this respect the opposite of a play like Sophocles's *Oedipus Rex*. Though the fates of the women inspire in us pity and terror we are not allowed to experience a catharsis and leave the theatre 'calm of mind, all passion spent'. Euripides's play is episodic: we witness a series of scenes involving the fates of different characters: Hecuba, Andromache, Astyanax, Cassandra. The action is effectively over when the play begins: Troy is defeated, the women waiting to learn their fate. Euripides's technique of recalling past events (through Hecuba's narrations) and anticipating others (through Cassandra's prophecies) is appropriate to epic rather than tragedy. We are made aware of wider, bigger issues than the merely personal. The destruction of an entire city, a whole civilisation is presented to us.

Bond, too, is concerned with a wider canvas: the fates of the individuals – whether the oppressors or the liberators – are subservient to the fate of the people. That the islanders shake off the tyranny of Greece as surely as the Trojans succumbed to it through their own political folly is what matters. It is vitally important for the continuation of our own species that we learn from the lesson of their history. Bond has structured his drama in two clear parts. Having established the epic form at the start he expands its potential gradually as the play unfolds. The first act culminates in the violence as the city is destroyed. The audience has been led to expect these events from their familiarity with the story and the mode of presentation. From Euripides's drama we anticipate the sacrifice of Astyanax as the climatic act of cruelty. But the first act ends not with this, but with a far more terrible event: Hecuba's blinding.

In Bond's drama the theme of Hecuba's learning about the world and accepting her political destiny and duty is central. It is only just beginning here, but even her desperation and wish to evade reality is far more important than the sacrifice of Astyanax. She is already reacting to events and this process will continue throughout the play. Hence the killing of the child is restricted to one off-stage scream and the suffering of Cassandra is cut short by Hecuba's entry. Bond has changed here the mother of Astyanax (it was Andromache) the more to deflect our attention from the tragedy of the individual to that of the state. In his '*Notes on Acting*' he further explains the importance of this shift of emotional emphasis:

> Perhaps we should say that most of the emotion occurs between the scenes and that the scenes show the consequences of these emotions. You can make a distinction between a blow and the consequences of a blow. Very few blows should be struck in the play because when they are struck they should be a knockout. So most of the blows occur before the scenes. The scene itself is the reeling effect of the blow.' (*The Woman*, p. 126)

We are prepared for the second act of the play which can move freely away from the material established in the first act and in so doing bring the audience, gripped by the unfolding of a Greek epic, face to face with the consequences of the previous action both for the characters and, more importantly, for themselves.

'*Restoration*'

Restoration is the most cunning of Bond's plays, a witty comedy of manners written by a Marxist playwright. Of course Bond's play is much more than this: it contrasts throughout the sophisticated world of the wealthy idle aristocracy with that of the bourgeois merchant and the worker. In an influential article written in *Scrutiny* in 1937, L.C. Knights had dismissed the comedy of the post-Restoration period as trival and dull. John Wain, applying the tyranny of left-wing dogma and critical of a drama reflective of an upper-class culture, had compared Congreve unfavourably with the author of *Charley's Aunt*. The new wave of theatre with a working-class setting which established itself at the Royal Court in the late 'fifties was suspicious of any undue concern with style. But by the mid 'sixties the fashion had altered: the age of *Hair* and Carnaby Street saw a comparable change in dramatic style as Pinter turned from comedy of menace to comedy of manners and playwrights such as Orton revealed the potential of witty social satire. Celebrated comedies of the past were revived: Noel Coward, relegated to an ignominious position in the fifties assumed the status of a classic and the dramas of the Restoration period returned to the stage. Pre-eminent in this revival of a neglected form was William Gaskill whose productions of Farquhar's *The Beaux's Strategem* and *The Recruiting Officer* at the National and of Congreve's *The Double Dealer* at the Royal Court paved the way for a major revaluation of the genre.

Bond's decision to adapt the features of this idiom to his own ends was a very careful and shrewd one. His play is called *Restoration* but it takes place in the eighteenth century. Bond is fully aware of the difference between the plays of Wycherley and Etherege written in the reign of Charles II immediately after the Restoration of the monarchy in 1660 and those of Farquhar written in the reign of Queen Anne. Farquhar's plays – and those of his contemporary Vanbrugh – are not concerned with the savage exposé of ruthless conduct characteristic of the earlier comedies; they anticipate the good-humoured urbanity and sentimentality of Goldsmith who was writing at the end of the eighteenth century. The aristocratic playgoers of the Restoration period gradually gave way to the new class of wealthy London merchants whose tastes were very different: instead of comedies centering on the twin themes of sex and money, both of which were handled with deadly seriousness, they demanded plays which were far removed from the commercial reality of their own lives and which did not show the cleverest man winning, but the most virtuous.

The fashion-conscious beau of Bond's play, Lord Are, is a figure from Vanbrugh: he has many of the characteristics of the Lord Foppington from *The Relapse*, a character played subsequently with great success by Simon Callow who created the role of Are. In *The Relapse* the greedy and affected Lord is outwitted by his brother and Miss Hoyden, the country girl both are pursuing for her fortune. This play was particularly popular at the end of the eighteenth century as Sheridan adapted it as *A Trip To Scarborough*. But the geniality of Vanbrugh, Sheridan and Goldsmith is quite lacking in Bond's treatment. Are is a figure from earlier comedy with all the cunning and ruthlessness that is the corollary of his wit. He is more like Dorimant, Etherege's Man of Mode who outwits all his rivals to be rid of his mistress and win the hand of a wealthy heiress. The play, whilst promising a happy ending along the lines of eighteenth century romantic comedy, frustrates the audience's expectations by reverting to a dénouement in key with seventeenth-century standards of dramatic propriety. Bond's drama is in effect a comment on sentimentality and evasion of truth. Augustan sentiments such as:

> God bless the squire and his relations
> And keep us in our proper stations

he sees as falsity. He asks us to reject the sham of our present social system as surely as he rejects an improbable romantic ending to his story. If we wish in life as in the theatre to avoid reality then we must expect to pay the price.

The first scene establishes neatly the situation of the play which is firmly in the tradition of the comedy of manners. It opens with Lord Are intent on arranging his appearance to win over Ann, the wealthy heiress of Mr Hardache. Like Aimwell and Archer in *The Beaux's Stratagem* he is a fortune hunter, but as the aggressive poseur who compares the country unfavourably to the town – a theme which runs throughout Restoration comedy – he more closely resembles Vanbrugh's Lord Foppington:

ARE: Wha-ha! I must not laugh, it'll spoil my pose. Damn! the sketch shows a flower. 'Tis too late for the shops, I must have one from the ground.

FRANK: What kind sir?

ARE: Rip up that pesky little thing on the path. That'll teach it to grow where gentlemen walk. (FRANK offers the flower.) Smell it! If it smells too reprehensible throw it aside. I hate the gross odours the country gives off. 'Tis always in a sweat! Compare me to the sketch.

FRANK: (*checks sketch*) Leg a bit more out.

ARE: Lawd I shall be crippled. *Do* they stand about the country so? When I pass the boundaries of the town I lower the blinds in mourning and never go out on my estate for fear of the beasts. (*Restoration* pp. 7–8).

The key to Bond's skill in this play is the way in which he is so fair and accurate in his presentation. Are is very funny, but the pastiche of this style cuts a great deal deeper. As the dramatists of the immediate post-Restoration period observed, both a witty manner and an elegant deportment were signs not only of breeding but of intelligence. Wit implies both verbal ingenuity and mental skill. It is the cleverest men who are always the winners in the plays of Wycherley and Congreve. This success is independent of conventional standards of morality: it creates its own laws.

When the dramatists of the eighteenth century ignored this intransigent reality and presented the working out of financial and emotional issues dependent more on good fortune or good breeding they took the sting out of the Comedy of Manners and created a drama which was not an accurate reflection of the age. Bond recognises this: his villain is witty, clever and amoral. But what is for Are a reasoned attitude to life is not accepted by the dramatist as a rational way of organising society.

Hardache and Ann seem at first to be characters from Goldsmith. Hardache has all the geniality of Hardcastle in *She Stoops To Conquer* and Ann, though nothing like Kate Hardcastle, is very like her mother whose longing to escape from the country to London is ridiculed by the dramatist. Hardache is just such a character as Steele's Mr Sealand in *The Conscious Lovers*: an example of the rising merchant class which was taking over from the landed aristocracy at the end of the seventeenth century. At first he appears Are's dupe, unaware that his daughter is marrying a young lord who had debts to honour and is penniless. But Hardache, contemptuously dismissed by Are as 'iron founder, ship builder, mine owner and meddler and merchant in men and much else that hath money in it' proves to be as cunning as his son-in-law. He will not protect the interests of the worker, Bob; and Rose will crucially underestimate that force which we recognise in Are's description as essentially the power of capital. Ann is no less unscrupulous: she is interested solely in her husband's position, hoping he will die and leave her a wealthy young widow. But she is his inferior in appearance and in cunning. Her ridiculous scheme of pretending to be a ghost first to frighten him into taking her to London and then to scare him to death pitifully misfires as he runs his sword through her. She is no match for her husband whose style and ingenuity are the complement to his wit, as we see in his shrewd assessment of Ann:

> ARE: Not uncomely, but the neglect is beyond redemption! Style cannot strike at any age like a conversion, its rudiments are learned in the nursery or never. That redness of cheek might be had off a coster's barrow for ha'pence. But I'll take her, as she comes with money. (*Restoration*, p. 11.)

When Are later has the upper-hand in the marriage his witty refusal to keep his part of the bargain strikes a more fundamental truth in the play. Such a paradox as: 'Why, ma'am if a gentleman kept his promises society would fall apart' is an irony which conveys Bond's own message.

The marriage of Are and Ann is a union of landed aristocratic arrogance and capital. This union constitutes the oppressor of the working people who Bond, in the earlier part of the play, portrays as labourers, little better than animals. 'Treat me like an animal and I'll be one', says Frank and uses this as justification for his theft of the silver. His own rebellious conduct will lead him to the same prison and the same scaffold as the honest Bob, who is the scapegoat for Are's murder of his wife. At least Frank dies unrepentant as he had lived: in a series of powerful stage images we see him tied up like a beast when exhausted by work, caged, and then escape to live a life of drinking and whoring. Society has made him like this; nor is the honest Bob any better. Like his mother, he accepts his position, sentimentally trusting in the benevolence of the man for whom he will be sacrificed. When Bob's mother discovers Frank has stolen the spoons her cry of: 'My silver gone! I polished it for years!' has cutting satiric force. It is she who in this society is the possession, a function she accepts as completely as the parson whose pious concern for the stolen goods further emphasises the irony:

PARSON: This woman learns of a lifetime of wasted labour. The cherished things on which she lavished her affection are gone. How will she occupy the time she would have devoted to cleaning them? (*Restoration* p. 39)

Bond's merciless exposé of Bob's absurd servility at the end of the act when, in reply to Are's: 'Bob, throw the toast to the hens on your way to prison' he '*weeping, picks up the toast rack and nods*' is matched by the telling image of his mother later in the play ingenuously accepting the pardons from Are and assiduously burning them at his instruction:

MOTHER: Kind of him. Save me fetch the kindlin'. Official pretty crown on top. Cut them out for Christmas decoration. (*Shakes her head*). Best do what yoo're towd. Bob was learning to read. (*Tears the papers*) Ont start that doo yoo ont git the work out the way. (*Restoration* p. 89)

Rose is a very different figure with a natural wit that sees straight to the heart of things. She is appalled at the complacent attitude of Bob and his mother and speaks out in his defence. She is shrewd enough to know that to defeat Are she must play by his rules. She has learnt this from her mother, a black slave, whose advice she puts to good use when she helps Frank escape. She sees further than the other servants, realising that if Are is convicted of the murder, Ann's money will go back to her father. As she expresses it tersely: 'It's not between Are and Bob. It's between two bosses.' She attempts to enlist Hardache's help; but she has underestimated – as Bond encourages the audience to do – his mercenary cunning. The benevolent father is seen in his true colours for the first time when he meets Are in prison and uses Rose's information to blackmail his son-in-law into giving him what he wants.

Here Bond craftily employs the features of Restoration comedy – in its urbanity of style and the exposure of the pecuniary motives this masks – to give us a sharply defined picture of the economic bases on which both this society and our own function:

HARDACHE: I don't like interfering – but she was my daughter and she'd want the right man to hang.

ARE: (*Calm and precise*) Why here at such a time?

HARDACHE: Where better? All parties to hand. If questions have to be asked they can answer them directly. And if you have to take lodgings on the prison next door – you're spared the extra journey.

ARE: Sir. My drinking companion the Lord Lieutenant – in whose bosom my hand lies deeper than ever the dearly beloved disciple's lay in Christ's – will not let you clap me in gaol. Tomorrow I am promised for the races, and 'twould quite spoil his party.

HARDACHE: Son-in-law. Your title gives you acquaintance, money gives me mine. I pay for the coach that takes your mighty friend to the races. Here's a riddle: why does a sensible man like me let his daughter marry a fop like you?

ARE: Fop? A fella don't boast but –

HARDACHE: Coal.

ARE: I misheard.

HARDACHE: No. Under your land.

ARE: I have been rooked.

HARDACHE: Your title cost me a packet but I meant to pay for it with your coal. The marriage made it mine.

> Or my grandson's – I think ahead for the good of the
> firm. The firm'll do very nicely out of thee and me.
> Now this mishap upsets my grand scheme. (pp. 74-5)

He therefore proposes another agreement which means
that Bob is again sacrificed to a further alliance of authority
and power. As Bob hands over his pen for the two to sign
what is in effect his death warrant his comment 'Expect a
pardon look like that' has a chilling theatrical irony.

It is Rose who is again compelled to take the initiative
and it is her scene with Old Lady Are which draws from
Bond his most sustained Restoration parody. The opening
lines in which she complains of her maid having put the
decanter out of her reach echo Congreve's introduction to
Lady Wishfort in *The Way Of The World*. But Lady Are is
every bit as selfish as her son; she has none of the folly of
Lady Wishfort. What this interview exposes – through an
employment of the high style of Restoration comedy – is
that justice, honesty, and pathos are powerless in the face
of the arrogant assurance of power and wealth. It is a
fundamental theme of the Comedy of Manners which
presents a character like Mrs Loveit in *The Man of Mode*
entirely at the mercy of Dorilant when she is foolish enough
to bare her heart to him, or delights in the confounding of a
pair of criminals like Congreve's Marwould and Fainall by
their more cunning rivals. When Rose kneels and says 'I
beg you' Lady Are retorts with all the hauteur of Oscar
Wilde's Lady Bracknell: 'Get up child. A thing is not made
more impressive by being said by a dwarf.' We are made to
see that justice resides in the hands of this wilful old
woman, who, when Rose has left in anger, suddenly
changes her mind out of spite towards her son.

Unlike Lady Are's maid Dorothea, who the old woman
tells us would have waited for the guinea offered her

instead of losing her temper and leaving without it, Rose is not an opportunist. She learns from her experiences and at the end of the play triumphantly emerges as an agent who will effect change. Nor is this awareness sudden or arbitrary since Bond has throughout the play employed a startlingly original technique which enriches his presentation of the *mores* of another period. The play's setting is: 'England, eighteenth century – or another place at another time'. It is no mere irony that Lady Are should say: 'I am an old woman with an empty glass and there is nothing to think of that does not wring me with regret for the past, convulse me at the follies of the present, or make me tremble before what is to come.' Bond wastes no sympathy on her since his interpretation of history forsees her extinction and that of her class. Bond sees his characters both within the context of their own age and out of it and he matches this observation with a telling theatrical device whereby all the workers in the play are given songs in which this awareness is expressed. Though the oppressors in the play have the greatest intelligence and wit they cannot see beyond their own situation. A broader perspective is vouchsafed only to Bob, Frank, Rose and Bob's Mother, the victims of the system dramatised within the play. Though Bob and his mother are victims who will their own servitude by a passive acceptance of it, in the wider canvas of the piece – through the many interpolated songs – they share the viewpoint of Frank and Rose. This viewpoint is seen to be more accurate historically whilst its realisation in theatrical terms is more expressive. In some respects Bond learnt how to give his work this more complex texture through his collaboration with Henze: both the extensive employment of music and the complexity of vision realised in the powerful images of these songs opens up the potential of the dramatic medium.

The song: 'The Gentleman', performed by Bob and Rose

immediately after Are has insisted in a perfectly reasonable way that if Bob is not hanged 'anarchy must triumph', opens up the implications of any passive acceptance of tyranny and encourages us to reject any act of kindness from an oppressor. Bond will take this up as the central theme of *Summer*; here the song functions in a very similar way to the poem *Pompei* discussed earlier. After a series of details recounting the courtesy of a soldier: 'He steps out of the way to let her pass . . .' 'he takes the child and holds it on his shoulder' we reach the shock of: 'At the door of the gas chamber/He hands the child back to her arms'.

In the songs throughout the play Bond employs anachronisms of this sort which alert us to the contemporary relevance of his theme whilst showing us a class more conscious of its own destiny. Frank's 'Song of Learning' functions in sharp contrast to his character within the story to show us a man who is representative of this consciousness: he is no longer the individual, but a voice of the people:

> For fifty thousand years I fought in their wars
> I died so often I learned how to survive
> For fifty thousand years I fought battles to save their wealth
> That's how I learned to know the enemy myself.
>
> For fifty thousand years I gave them my life
> But in all that time they never learned how to live
> For fifty thousand years I was governed by men of wealth
> Now I have learned to make the laws I need for myself.
> (p. 20)

Rose is the key link between these songs and the action of

the play; she is the one character who learns through experience. In the highly poetic speech which opens the final scene she describes her vision of London. It is a horrific vision of slavery where 'men walk the streets with chains hanging from their mouths', recalling the life from which her mother escaped but equally relevant to the contemporary scene as described by Blake in his poem *London*:

> I wander through each chartered street
> Near where the chartered Thames doth flow
> And mark in every face I meet
> Marks of weakness, marks of woe.

Rose asks: 'What have I learned?' and replies 'If nothing, then *I* was hanged'. Her climactic song, before she turns and crosses the river, is significantly entitled: 'Man Is What He Knows' and concludes:

> 'Wind and rain cannot tell where
> they blow
> but we may know who we
> are and where we go.' (p. 100)

It is Bond's assertion of hope for the future which has been powerfully realised within the complex structure of this drama.

'Summer'

In terms of dramatic form and theatrical style *Summer* – Bond's second play for the National Theatre – is totally different from anything he had written before. It concerns

79

four people: Xenia and her daughter, Ann who are visiting Marthe and her son, David. The setting is 'The Present'; the location 'Eastern Europe'. The opening scene edges the audience gently into the personal worlds of these four people through their inconsequential chatter: a technique of narrative exposition familiar from the plays of Ibsen, but quite new for Bond. He shows as consummate a command of this idiom as he did of the style of Greek epic or Restoration comedy: we are interested in these characters as individuals, gripped too by the element of mystery, anxious to learn for instance, the reason for the visit or the precise nature of the relationship between Ann and David. In the second scene the mystery deepens. We are very much in the theatrical world of Ibsen as Xenia informs Martha that Ann 'knows too much about the past'; we too wish to share their secrets. When we hear of the arrest of Ann's grandfather and of his subsequent imprisonment the situation holds out all the promise of *The Wild Duck* in which we gradually discover more and more about the disgrace of Hedvig's grandfather, Ekdal, and hints at significant events in the past such as those which are gradually dragged to the surface in *Ghosts* or which live on in the gloom-laden environment of *Rosmersholm*.

When, later in this scene, David launches unprompted into his uninterrupted medical description of the symptoms of his mother's cancer the dramatic promise appears to be fulfilled, but his speech, so clinical and complex is a far cry from the veiled euphemisms of Doctor Rank in *A Doll's House* or Mrs Alving's confession to Oswald. David's apparent harshness in relating these facts not for Xenia's benefit but for his mother's, in order to force her to face reality, shifts the drama off its naturalistic axis, preparing us for the ethical discussion which is to follow. In the next scene friendly chatter between Ann and Marthe soon gives way to Marthe's discussion of one of the fundamental political issues with which the drama will deal. In response to Ann's question as to what her mother was like at her age Marthe answers: 'Very kind. All her family were. They owned half the town. That isn't a figure of speech. Factories, a bank, the local paper, the farms in the hills,' and she goes on to explain the implications of this. She expounds a fundamental thesis of Bond that kindness does not change the world and that tenderness and goodwill are irrelevent if the organisation of society is basically iniquitous:

> Your family made the people who loved and respected them confuse kindness with justice. That is corrupting. You can live without kindness, you can't live without justice – or fighting to get it. If you try to you're mad. You don't understand yourself or the world.' (*Summer*, p. 20)

Bond's political viewpoint is more radical than Ibsen's but ethical discussions of this sort do occur in the work of the Norwegian dramatist. As Shaw pointed out, it was Ibsen who substantially changed the formula of the nineteenth century drama:

> Formerly you had in what was called a well-made play an exposition in the first act, a situation in the second, an unravelling in the third. Now you have exposition situation and discussion; and the discussion is the test of the playwright.' (Shaw: *The Quintessence of Ibsenism*, p. 87)

In *Summer* we have already had the exposition; now we move into a description by Marthe and Xenia of those events in their past which have shaped their lives and of which Ann is ignorant. We learn of the fact that during the war the local islands were requisitioned by the Germans who paid Xenia's father rent to use them as a concentration camp and of how Xenia used her position to save Marthe when she was about to be shot as a hostage. The situation is complicated by the fact that after the war there was a revolution in which Xenia's father was arrested and imprisoned on evidence given by Marthe whilst Xenia escaped to England. These revelations and the moral dilemma they imply disturb Ann who says: 'Let me think about what you've both told me', whilst her mother comments: 'Yes think. And learn what people do in this world.' The situation is markedly similar to that at the end of the second act of *Mrs Warren's Profession* where Vivie learns of her mother's past and is obliged to revise her opinions. Like Shaw, Bond is writing a problem play in the Ibsen mould but his techniques are more savage and his political aim more extreme.

In the next scene we shift to the islands and are brought into a closer confrontation with those events already described by Xenia and Marthe. We meet a new character, a German, who is also reliving his past and has returned for a holiday to the very place in which he served as a soldier. He is one of the most sinister characters Bond has ever created, a clever device to draw us more completely into the horrors of the extermination camps which he describes with a mixture of nostalgia and regret. He constantly protests his innocence: 'This wasn't a concentration camp. We were private soldiers: not officers, not Gestapo, not guilty'. In Bond's skilful hands his exculpatory narrative serves to incriminate him more and more. Though the German disclaims responsibility for the final horrors – 'We were not criminals. We'd done everything in the open.

According to the laws of war. Harsh – but war is harsh' – Bond brings home the full obscenity of the situation by a reference to the action recreated in *We Come To The River*: 'The public address system played dance music to keep spirits high. We came with marches and left with waltzes.' It is the German's justification of Nazism in that common-place theory which is anethema to Bond – that men are by nature vile and that it is therefore vital to protect our cultural heritage – which ultimately damns him;

> GERMAN: Men are animals. We can't be trusted with another man's wife or his money. Not even with our own daughters. No-one's safe on our streets at night. If we don't get our fodder we whine. What saves us from ourselves? Culture. The standards of our fathers. They struggled for centuries to make them strong . . . That's why we went to war.' (*Summer*, p. 25)

More significantly this justification also incriminates Xenia for in the middle of it the German refers to 'the girl in white' who symbolised the faith of the occupying forces. This mysterious figure – a symbol in the style of Ibsen – was Xenia as a girl. In the next two scenes of the play it is the woman who will be forced to come to terms with her past in a confrontation with the implications of her conduct and life.

By bringing the subject of the Nazi death camps into a play which initially promised to be a domestic drama concerned with the tragic death of one of the characters, Bond has further applied his strategy of employing bourgeois theatrical conventions to fulfil the purposes of the political dramatist. Into the framework of this problem play he has brought the subject matter handled by Peter

Weiss in *The Investigation* or Ralph Hochhuth in *The Representative*. He is much closer to Weiss than Hochhuth whose naturalistic drama set partially in Auschwitz, concentrates on the psychological and spiritual agony of a Catholic priest drawn into a sympathetic stand with the Jews. Weiss by contrast, never mentions the word 'Jew' once in his play: his rigorously austere piece of epic theatre in which a series of anonymous victims and criminals relate dispassionately the horrors of Auschwitz emphasises the culpability of the whole system: that every clerk and railway worker who assisted in the transportation of prisoners was as guilty as those in charge of the camp. Bond shares this view and relates these details not with the intention of overwhelming us with emotional horror. His aim is different from that of Peter Barnes in his more Artaudian piece *Laughter* which, like Bond's play, begins deceptively – as a situation comedy set in an office on Christmas Eve – but which moves into a description and representation of events in Auschitz consequent on the revelation that the workers are processing orders of Cyclone B for use in the gas chambers. Bond's political point is more precise than Barnes': he sees Nazism and the inexorable extension of its logic in genocide as the inevitable consequence of capitalism and imperialism. As Marthe says in attacking what Xenia's class stood for: 'The confusion and competition led to such passion and madness that in the end there was war.' Moreover this attitude is international as Bond makes clear in a mordantly ironic poem accompanying the play:

> If Auschwitz had been in Hampshire
> There would have been Englishmen to guard it
> To administer records
> Work the gas ovens

And keep silent
The smoke would have drifted over these green hills.

Bond is again working out the consequences of a dramatic paradox similar to that employed in *Saved*, but here even more extreme. The ultimate horror is not the scenes of violence witnessed on the islands. What is worse is the system and philosophy which gives rise to it. And in the play it is Xenia's family who are therefore as much to blame as the Nazis whom they pretended to assist in order to betray their plans to the partisans. Xenia finds it impossible to understand how her father could have been arrested by the very partisan to whom he was betraying the Germans, but this irony is overshadowed by a greater one in that her kindness and her father's conduct were meaningless because – as Marthe points out – 'the foundations of your world were crooked and so everything in it was crooked.' The play finally forces the characters to face the past as Marthe spits at Xenia, thus recalling and avenging the women imprisoned with her who when she heard who Marthe worked for said 'If I could live to spit in her face' and spat in the dirt. Xenia's response: 'You carried a dead woman's spit round in your mouth for forty years' serves the more powerfully to drive home the force of this stage image which clinches the political argument expressed through Marthe. In the next scene the German sends a bouquet of flowers to the woman he has now recognised as the 'girl in white'; his tribute fixes in a complementary image the nature of Xenia's guilt. In the two short final scenes – the last one less than a page in length – we see the naturalistic tone re-establish itself as Marthe dies and Ann prepares to leave with her mother. The last dying fall is deceptive. The responses of the characters here are in the circumstances strange, not immediately explicable. The young people admit they love each other and therefore they must part; Marthe, in saying to them: 'I die so that you might live' uses her death to show the meaning of her life. It is we, the audience, who must leave the theatre more aware of the events that they have relived and confronted, for Bond has made us realise that what we have witnessed is not only their past, but our own.

4
Tragedy And Comedy

On Being an Optimist: a Wall Poem

There's a solution to every problem
The solving of which would make the world better

But to do one thing right
You may need to do
Four things wrong
Don't let the four things
Stop the one thing

And though you lived in a time
When for one right thing
A hundred wrongs have to be done
Seize the chance!
Do the one thing!
Or the things that are wrong
Will be one hundred and one.

(*Theatre Poems and Songs* p. 107)

Bond's versatility in his employment of different theatrical styles is an indication of the significance of dramatic form in his writing. From the start of his career Bond set himself against tragedy and the type of tragicomedy which has established itself as a dominant dramatic genre in the post-war theatre. As he has developed he has forged an original dramatic medium which combines epic theatre and his own version of tragicomedy. It is worth examining the latter at this point since his rejection of the tragic in drama is the corollary of his rejection of a nihilistric attitude to life. He has turned his back on the fashionable despair of the Absurdists which Pinter and Stoppard have explored in their creation of a type of existential comedy, and he has little sympathy with the intensity of the emotional satire which characterises the work of a writer like Peter Barnes. His breadth of political perspective gives him a vision which can see beyond individual human issues both to a more accurate vision of corruption and the remedy for it. In this he again resembles Shaw who dismissed the 'tinpot little tragedies' of personal crisis – such as his heroine's despair in Act II of *Major Barbara* – and concentrated on the method of building a new world out of the ruins of the old. Shaw's Devil in *Man and Superman*: says:

> This marvellous force of Life of which you boast is a force of Death: man measures his strength by his destructiveness . . . It is the same in everything. The highest form of literature is the tragedy, a play in which everybody is murdered at the end. (*Man and Superman*, pp. 102-3)

Shaw would have none of this and nor will Bond. Shaw reserved his greatest contempt for the type of fashionable melodrama by writers such as Sardou and Pinero which

1. Dennis Waterman in *Saved* at the Royal Court Theatre, 1965.

2. The final tableau of *Saved*, in the 1969 revival, Royal Court Theatre, with Kenneth Cranham as Ken.

3. *Narrow Road to the Deep North*, Royal Court Theatre, 1969.

4. *Early Morning*, 1969, Royal Court Theatre, Shirley Ann Field as Florence and Moira Redmond as Queen Victoria.

5. *Lear*, Royal Court Theatre, 1971. Harry Andrews as Lear.

6. *The Sea*, Royal Court Theatre, 1973. Coral Browne as Mrs Rafi.

7. *Bingo*, Royal Court Theatre, 1974. John Gielgud as Shakespeare, Arthur Lowe as Ben Jonson.

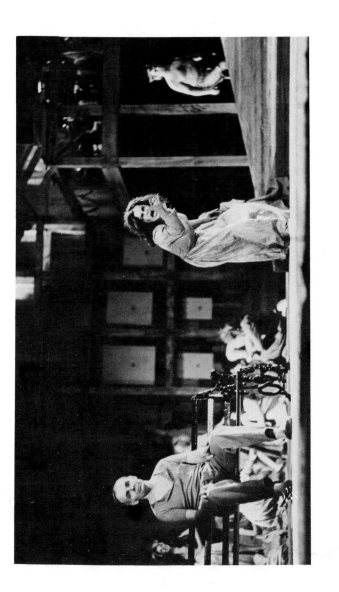

8. *We Come to the River*, The Royal Opera House, 1976.

9. *The Woman*, The National Theatre, 1978. Yvonne Bryceland as Hecuba, Dinah Stabb as Cassandra, Nicky Henson as Heros

10. *The Worlds*, the Royal Court Theatre, 1979. Performed by the Royal Court Young People's Theatre Scheme.

11. Simon Callow as Lord Are in *Restoration*, 1981. Royal Court Theatre.

showed a resolution of emotional problems in the convenient suicide of the heroine at the end. For Bond the *bête
noire* is not so much the tragedy, a dramatic form rendered
virtually extinct by the erosion of faith and confidence in a
world reeling from the discoveries of Freud, Marx and
Einstein, but the type of tragicomedy created and refined
by Beckett.

In a revealing attack on the critics of Howard Brenton's
play *Romans in Britain* published in *The Guardian*, Bond
made the reasons for his rejection of Beckett clear:

> Of course not all dramatists are socialists. Beckett is said
> to have made liberal – even capitalist – culture possible.
> He is said to have shown that however you degrade
> people an unquenchable spark of humanity remains in
> them – and therefore we are not animals but may still
> hope to build a humane society. Experience in concen-
> tration camps is often offered as proof of this. In them
> many victims subjected to ultimate degradations still
> retain the human spark. Unfortunately the argument is
> false. Those who ran the camps did not retain it. The
> terrible truth is that human beings may lose all vestage of
> humanity and become monsters. In our age we may look
> into the face of men who are not men. This truth has
> silenced the artist Beckett. It silences or trivialises all
> writers who follow his shadow.   And if the theory of
> the spark were true – how would that guide us through
> the desperately needed reorganisation of society, or
> teach us to express our humanity in the changing world?
> It is as if Beckett told us to be comforted because in the
> lungs of the corpse there is still a pocket of air. What use
> is that to the living? What teaching is that for the young?
> (*The Romans* and the Establishment's Figleaf: *Guardian*
> November 3rd 1980)

Bond's determination to create a more positive, useful alternative to this type of theatre has resulted in his own brand of tragicomedy which has a form and logic to match his own very different ethical viewpoint.

'Saved'

Just as the discoveries of Darwin and Marx served to mould Shaw's evolutionary socialism, so Bond's Marxism is the basis for his critique of society and for his reconstruction of a new one. Like Shaw Bond is a rational thinker, not a romantic. His focus is on man in society not on man as an individual. The paradox which informs so much of his work is summed up in his statement: 'Like most people I am a pessimist by experience, but an optimist by nature': he believes in the perfectability of humanity given the right social environment. This attitude informs *Saved*, a drama which Bond has described in terms of tragicomedy: 'By not playing his traditional role in the tragic Oedipus pattern of the play, Len turns it into what is formally a comedy'. (*Plays: One*, p. 301) Bond's drama is not a haphazard amalgamation of comic and tragic effects; he in no way shares the philosophical view which informs Ionesco's aesthetic: 'It seems to me that the comic is tragic, and the tragedy of man is pure derision' (*Notes and Counternotes* p. 27) Bond is in some respects neoclassical in his careful establishing of a contrast of tragic and comic features which develop towards a tragic climax that is then placed and modified within a wider perspective.

The first scene of the play is richly comic and yet serves both to define the negative social situation and present Len's sexual insecurity. He cannot make love to Pam until Harry is out of the house; later the old man will find him in a compromising situation with his wife. 'The Oedipus outcome', Bond states, 'should be a row and a death'. Though' the murder of the baby shows the Oedipus atavistic fury fully unleashed', Len does not take part in this. In the home there is a row, but Len is persistent; there follows the scene with Harry (Len with a knife in his hand; the old man in his night-shirt 'dressed as a ghost') in which someone other than Len is helpful and frank. Bond emphasises: 'The only sensible object in defeating an enemy is to make him your friend. That happens in this play, although in fact most social and personal problems are solved by alienation or killing'. Len's tenacity, expressed most potently in the image of him mending the chair in the final scene, is the basis of Bond's presentation of hope for a better life. It is all too easy to concentrate on the personal and emotional issues – the stoning of the baby, the family row, the isolation of the four characters in the final scene – and thus to see the play as pessimistic and tragic. This is not Bond's intention. His reason for optimism resides in the resilience, sensitivity and ability to learn which is manifested by Len but which represents a deeper faith in humanity and a fundamental desire to live in a sane and rational society.

'The Three Sisters'

Writing about the dénouement of *Saved* Bond said:

> If the spectator thinks this is pessimistic that is because he has not learned to clutch at straws. Clutching at straws is the only realistic thing to do. The alternative, apart from the self-indulgence of pessimism, is fatuous optimism based on superficiality of both feeling and observation. (*Plays, One*, p. 309)

The same attitude informs his approach to Chekhov, another writer of tragicomedy, who was the subject of Bond's work when he translated a version of *The Three Sisters* for the Royal Court in 1966. This came between the writing of *Saved* and *Early Morning* and serves to clarify Bond's view of the mixed dramatic genre. *The Three Sisters* was Chekhov's penultimate play; it dramatises the clash of social values within the Prozorov household consequent upon Andrey's marriage to a bourgeois *arriviste*, Natasha. It may be argued that Chekhov's sympathies are wholly with the sisters whose cultural and ethical standards are far superior to those of their sister-in-law. Whilst Bond can have little sympathy with the élitist class who were to be swept away by the Russian revolution of 1917 and whose culture was to be replaced by a Marxist one, their humanitarian attitude to the victims of the fire – in pointed contrast to Natasha's impersonal approach to charity – has affinities with Len's instinctive goodness. The ironic contrast of the unhappy Vershinin and the ebullient Tusenbach, the former a natural optimist and the latter profoundly pessimistic, is in key with Bond's attitude as an optimistic by nature and a pessimist by experience. Undoubtedly he was drawn to the play because of its social and political message: it is the play of Chekhov which most acutely foreshadows the Revolution and is at the same time – as Robert Brustein has pointed out – the one most concerned with the crucial role played by environment in the lives of the characters. There is also an irony in the fact that – like *Saved* – the original reception of the play was not what the author intended. Chekhov, according to Stanislavsky, was amazed at the first reading of the play by the Moscow Art Theatre because, in the producer's words: 'He had written a happy comedy and all of us considered the play a tragedy and even wept over it.'

Chekhov's attitude is explicable if we see the conduct of the sisters at the end of Act IV precisely that of 'clutching at straws' . . . the only realistic thing to do'. By this point they have all experienced tragedy: Masha has lost Vershinin, Olga is trapped in a job she loaths and Irene's prospective husband has been killed in a duel. For many critics the optimism of the three at the play's close is false, but it is a precise example of the rational attitude to life Bond upholds. They are finally facing the truth. They will never return to their beloved Moscow and they must make the best of the situation. It is this awareness that gives them an unexpected new strength, the type of revelation which changes the lives of many subsequent characters in Bond's own drama. As he has explained in greater detail:

> Clutching at straws isn't a way of life. It's just a mark of determination. But you can only do this at the few low moments. You can't go on doing it. Find out what the situation is, don't fudge the issues, don't be depressed if it demands more of you than you'd hoped, don't pretend the situation is what it isn't – and the integrity with which you do this will be the basis of the energy you bring to changing the situation. (Letter to the author: 4.8.84.)

In his translation, he is concerned to emphasise the reality of the situation and to eradicate any false emotion or hint of spiritual sentiment. In his version Masha says: 'We're alone . . we must start again . . *We must stay alive* . . *We must stay alive*', expressions slightly more extreme in their emphasis on clutching at straws than 'we are left alone to begin our life over again. *We must live* . .' which is how Ann Dunnigan translates this in the Signet edition. A focus on the down-to-earth and the practical makes Bond have Irena say: 'One day people will know what all this is for, what all this suffering is for, *and nothing will be hidden*' as against Dunnigan's 'A time will come when everyone will know what all this is for, why there is all this suffering, *and there will be no mysteries*'. Whilst in Olga's speech which follows, instead of her saying: 'happiness and peace will come to this earth, and then they will remember kindly and *bless* those who are living now', Bond's version has 'Joy and peace will return to the world. They will look back at those who live now with kindness, and *thank* us' (italics mine) These changes of emphasis, though they may appear very minor, are clear indication of Bond's desire to place the eventual outcome of the play on an absolutely clear basis and are consistent with his overall aim as a tragicomic dramatist.

'Early Morning'

Undoubtedly Bond's funniest play to date is *Early Morning*, another tragicomedy in which the two extremes of the genre have been more completely exaggerated. The savagery of Bond's satire is expressed in scenes which vary from the mock trial of a couple who have killed and eaten a man in a cinema queue to a cannibalistic heaven presided over by Queen Victoria. Yet both these scenes are intensely comic. The play has been little performed since it incurred the wrath of the Lord Chamberlain in 1968; the intensity of the violence, the complex story and the lack of any realistic characterisation are problems which conventional actors find very difficult to cope with. On reading, the play can all too easily emerge as a rather self-indulgent inconsequential farrago of effects written by a novice out of his depth with the theatrical medium. Nothing could be further from the truth. Unhappy with the play, and puzzled by it on reading, I decided to mount a production of it with my students. We discovered that the moment you stop reading the play as a literary or dramatic text and see it in terms of the stage it is immediately apparent that Bond knows exactly what he is doing. Instead of extravagance we appreciate economy, instead of experiencing bewilderment we encounter a plot which is unfolded with consummate skill and clarity.

Mounting the play was a most useful exercise in the semiology of the stage. The way we read the drama in terms of performance profoundly influences interpretation, clarifies significance, in contrast to the limited and misleading impression we glean from analysing the text. This is, of course, true of any play, but it is acutely the case here, for *Early Morning* is a complex, highly original, piece of theatre handled by a playwright who knows how to provide the most telling pointers for his audience. Bond in fact revised the play for the publication in Methuen's collection. *Bond. Plays: One.* He did not change much, but the alternations reveal a theatrical craftsman correcting his work so as to give it the maximum clarity and expressiveness. A number of short sentences not essential to the unfolding of the action are pruned: the most outrageous comments of the Lord Chamberlain in scene 9 for instance, and such cries as Victoria's: 'I'll let you do all the amputations!' to Florence at the end of scene 12. There is a revealing addition: Len's brief soliloquy at the end of scene 8, that serves to clarify the action. Bond also restores the original order of the sequence of events in scene 8 and 9 which Gaskill had persuaded him to alter on grounds of expediency in the first production.

Since *Early Morning* is both a much neglected and much misunderstood drama it is useful to reassess its originality and success as a play crucial to a full understanding of Bond's work. The first feature which is immediately perceptible in performance – much less so in reading the text – is the clarity and importance of the narrative; this culminates in a trio of ingeniously devised scenes of farce, one in each part of the play. Bond also utilizes a series of vivid stage images which serve to focus our attention on the key moments in the drama. In this work Bond first experimented with anachronism which is employed throughout, both in brief flashes and more extended sequences: a technique which serves to point up the relevance of the play to our own age as well as to provide a cutting humour. This aspect of Bond's satire is paralleled by an extensive use of parody. The whole play is spiced with the author's particular brand of wit which expresses itself most incisively in the devices of epigram and paradox.

Bond makes it clear from the brief directions prefacing the play that it falls into certain clearly defined sections. The first part occupies scenes 1 to 5 in which we see an attempted *coup d'état* thwarted by the cunning of Victoria herself. Disraeli and Prince Albert are in league against the Queen and attempt to enlist the support of Prince Arthur. In the opening conversation Bond does not waste a word in conveying first the tension and then the details of the situation. This is exposition pared down to its most effective:

(A corridor in Windsor Castle. PRINCE ALBERT and DISRAELI come on).

ALBERT. (Looks around) This is safe.

DISRAELI. Victoria's going to announce the Prince of Wales's engagement. Victoria's not popular. She's frightened. She knows a royal wedding will pacify the people, so we must strike now. (*Plays: One* p. 139)

The audience is instantly made aware of the importance of narrative as against character portrayal, an emphasis which requires that the actors do not indulge in naturalistic techniques but put across the story clearly and swiftly; an objective epic approach is called for. This conversation also establishes the way in which Bond will manipulate history to his own ends; the shock of seeing these two respected figures conspiring in a corridor (in our production we set the scene in a lavatory) makes it clear we must be alert to the shifts of perspective Bond will produce through his juggling of known and invented fact. In this context the function of the narrative is doubly important: as the continued line we follow through the many convolutions of the story, and as the framework upon which a sequence of significant images is super-imposed.

As advice to us on the production Bond sent me a letter which contained this remark:

> But remember, keep the play moving – keep everything as sharp as a colour film that reminds you of a black-and-white one. Encourage the audience to accept the logic of what is happening: two and two doesn't become closer to four the more you stare at it or linger over it. (Letter to the author: 18.5.83)

When directing the play I soon began to appreciate the necessity of pacing the work in such a way that both the clarity of the developing action and the importance of particular details were kept in focus throughout. An example of this occurs in scene 2. Albert is trying to win over Arthur who is in bed with his brother. It is vital that he convince Arthur before George wakes up. But Albert's objective is periodically halted by lengthier speeches in which he explains his philosophy and in so doing acts as a vehicle for Bond's satire of this viewpoint. We found that by changing from a whispered to a spoken voice at these points the distinction between the 'black and white' and the 'colour' was clearly indicated without any break in the narrative flow of the scene. Because Victoria plans to marry George to Florence Nightingale, Disraeli and Albert plot to assassinate her by bribing a condemned prisoner, Len, with an offer of freedom. In Windsor Great Park the plot misfires. Knowing he plans to murder her, Victoria persuades Florence (who is now her lover) to poison Albert. Disraeli arrives to find Albert dead and George fatally wounded by the Queen who is aiming at Len with Albert's hunting rifle.

Another feature which becomes clearer in performance is that the action is seen through the eyes of Arthur. He is the central character, a focus for the events around him; the drama portrays his reactions to what he sees, tracing his development from bewilderment through despair to enlightened commitment. He is the subject of the first scene, the object of Albert's machinations in the second and the crucial witness of the trial in scene 3. Throughout the central section of the play (scenes 6 to 15) we see him change from incomprehension at what is going on around him to involvement as the escalating madness and violence of the world convinces him to destroy it. This development is in two parts with a break after scene 10 (which is the point at which Bond states the possibility of an extra interval). On the run with his dying brother, Arthur stumbles on his father's grave. Albert's ghost appears and urges him to kill Victoria but is frightened away by George who then dies. Arthur next comes upon a mob, led by Gladstone, who are lynching Len for his failure to kill Victoria. By feigning to have Porton Plague Arthur frightens the mob away and rescues Len. It is here that Bond's first major revision of the text occurs. Left alone, Len tells us of his plan to capitalise on his knowledge of the princes's whereabouts by informing first Victoria and then both Disraeli and Gladstone in turn. This results in the Queen and Florence going to a cave near Bagshot where the Royal family is ambushed. Disraeli is about to have them shot when his soldiers shoot him instead on the orders of Gladstone. The execution is resumed when Gladstone arrives but the Queen and company escape again when Gladstone drops dead of a heart attack.

Narrated coldly, these incidents have all the absurd logic of a farce. This is precisely Bond's point as he now goes on to show Arthur so deranged by this savage travesty of human behaviour that he plans a scheme of mass genocide. He arranges for a tug-of-war at Beachy Head in which everyone will take part. At Victoria's orders even the hospitals are emptied and everyone lines up. Victoria, recognising that he is mad, sees this as a convenient way of being rid of Arthur and his followers. But she has not bargained on the cunning of his scheme whereby as soon as her team have released the rope, they rush to the edge of the cliff to look down. The cliff gives way under their weight and everyone is killed. Only Arthur and Florence – who had held back – remain. Finally Arthur shoots himself. We then shift to the final section which takes place in Heaven. There all the characters are re-united. But Arthur is unhappy. He cannot bring himself to join them in eating one another and he thus disturbs the order of Heaven. Finally Victoria suffocates him and his family try to eat him. But they have difficulty in finding his head which Florence, in sympathy, is hiding. Alone with her, Arthur persuades Florence to abstain from cannibalism. The head is discovered and eaten by George. Finally Arthur's skeleton is placed in a coffin from which he ascends whilst the rest sit down to a meal.

The above synopsis should make it evident that though

this story is highly inventive and bizarre, in performance the events are both clear and inevitable. The audience is gripped by the story, wishing to know, as in a highly imaginative thriller, how the issues will be resolved. This narrative device is basic to our enjoyment of the work; it is the ploy by which our attention is held. Bond in effect – though in a highly unorthodox manner – observes the unity of action. The inexorable unfolding of the story is also a comment on the behaviour of the characters. Victoria's repressive regime must inevitably provoke unrest and assassination; the consequences of the failed coup gradually drive a sane man to madness and despair; whilst Bond's picture of heaven is a logical extension of Victorian morality.

Bond's satire is sharpened by three climactic scenes of tightly organised farce. The political machinations of the first part culminate in the assassination attempt of scene 5. The pace of events is very carefully calculated by Bond who shows the action opening out – from a corridor through a bedroom, then the throne room to Windsor Great Park – and at the same time speeding up. As Albert confidently ignores his hired assassins, ludicrously disguised as rustics, Victoria takes Florence on one side and, in terms of intimate sexual endearment as the two call one another Victor and Freddie respectively, persuades Florence to poison Albert with a powder from her ear-ring. When George asks Florence what she is doing he receives the curt reply: 'Lady's talk' from his mother. Albert pompously proposes the loyal toast, drinking from Florence's shoe, but to Victoria's consternation insists on passing it round 'like a loving cup'. Her refusal to drink – 'I've signed the pledge. I'm teetotal. Drink is the ruin of the country' – is an inspired piece of farcical improvisation cut short by Lord Mennings snatching the shoe in an excess of fetishistic fervour. This is the signal for Len to whip out a pistol and cover the Queen. Since Arthur is blocking Len's aim, Albert frantically encourages him to shoot whilst pretending to disarm him. Meanwhile the 'rustics' are attempting unsuccessfully to contact base with a picnic hamper converted to a radio receiver. Events simultaneously reach a farcical climax as Victoria finishes off Albert by strangling him with the garter sash, Len finds his accomplices have tuned in to his favourite number on BBC Radio One by mistake and Disraeli arrives to discover all has not gone according to plan. A furious scuffle breaks out for the pistol Len has dropped in which George is shot by mistake. Victoria leaves with Florence and Disraeli returns with soldiers as the scene gradually winds down. The final stage direction for the dying Mennings is 'diminuendo'.

The signifying feature of this scene is its tempo. Bond is presenting us with a grotesque microcosm of the political state. The frenetic lunacy of this is matched by the coldly relentless plot and counter-plot of part two which comes to a head in the cave near Bagshot (scene 10). There is an almost mechanical precision here characteristic of farce, which we are led to anticipate through Len's expository soliloquy at the end of scene 8. The shooting in this scene is done by a firing squad who meticulously carry out a complex series of orders and counter-orders, pointing their rifles first at Arthur then – under Disraeli's instructions – at the Queen, and finally – under Gladstone's – shooting Disraeli. This grimly programmed sequence of events is set against the zanier logic of Victoria's conduct as she exercises her power in a manner typical of Lewis Caroll's Red Queen. She commands George to come back to life and, having succeeded, resorts to prayer when confronted by Gladstone. At first it seems that her confidence is misplaced as she says 'Amen' and looks up to find nothing has happened. But no sooner has Arthur muttered ruefully: 'Her gift doesn't work in reverse. A pity – that would be more useful to a politician' than the inexorable logic asserts itself and Gladstone drops dead of a heart attack. Her faith in the strength of prayer to move mountains has been vindicated.

This trick of taking a basic tenet of Victorian belief and extending it to its ludicrous ultimate informs the whole of the final section of the play as Bond's irony culminates in his version of a rigorously organised cannibalistic heaven. At the climax of this last part of the drama occurs another scene which Bond here specifically describes as a farce. This centres on the desperate attempt to find the last remains of Arthur – his head – which Florence is hiding under her skirt. Florence's efforts to conceal it are made the more difficult by the amorous activities of Arthur which finally draw attention to his whereabouts. The whole of this far-fetched scene is shot through with the more mundane remarks of Victoria – 'You don't just lose a head' – and her endless practical advice, such as instruction to George that he recite the National Anthem backwards to calm his nerves. The final moments of the scene are punctuated by George rushing in and out as he eats the head, thereby reducing it to a skull: an image which both brings the logic of the play to its conclusion and serves as an ironic visual parallel to the gradually disintigrating state of his own corpse in the previous part of the drama.

The visual images which Bond superimposes on this fast-moving narrative heighten our perception of the play's meaning. They are not employed as symbols with some deeper hidden meaning; rather, as pointers to the significance of the action. The first image which hits us with the force of shock is the appearance of George and Arthur in scene 3: we realise here that they are siamese twins. At the end of scene 4, as Len and Joyce are moved out of the dock 'it is seen that they are handcuffed together'. This revelation has the most marked effect on Arthur who sees in their condition a parallel with his own. Neither he nor the audience appreciate the full significance of this until later. This occurs at the end of the second section of the play when Arthur, believing he has solved the problems of the world, shoots himself. At this point the ghosts of those he has killed rise and, as he confidently asserts that he has set them free, 'they move apart to reveal that they are joined together like a row of paper cut-out men'. The sight appals Arthur whose horror is intensified by what follows:

> GEORGE comes from the line of ghosts. He holds himself as if he were still attached to ARTHUR . . . GEORGE goes to ARTHUR. He bends down and starts to fasten himself to ARTHUR. ARTHUR shudders and groans.

This is a powerful climactic image, both an effective *coup de théâtre* and a means of alerting the audience to the central theme of the drama. George represents the institutionalised, socially responsible side of Arthur, the reverse of his own withdrawn, sympathetic character. His obsession in the second part of the play with finding out why Len committed murder comes partly from his own intuitive awareness that he too is conditioned and compromised by his environment. As he retreats into madness he sheds his responsibility and thinks he is freeing the world. This is further emphasised by the gradually disintegrating corpse of his brother which he carries with him, as it is reduced first to a skeleton, and then finally to 'only a skull and a few bones, like a ragged epaulette'. But in suicide he realizes he has achieved nothing: those he has killed are not in reality free and neither is he.

The intensity of Arthur's manic vision of his panacea for

the world's evils is presented in scene 10. The length of this scene – essentially a soliloquy – its static nature and its position immediately after the Bagshot scene at the start of the second part of the play's central section give it the force of a reflective slow movement in the hectic symphonic structure of the drama. The suddenness of Arthur's conversion here emphasises the more strongly the totality of his mania. This was a point missed at first by Peter Stein when he directed the play in Berlin. Bond told me that Stein asked him to elucidate this scene as it was unclear to him. When Bond pointed out that Arthur was mad, Stein admitted he had not realized this, a point which staggered Bond who asked him how anyone who thought Hitler was right and had invented his own version of the Final Solution could possibly be regarded as sane. 'Ah', replied Stein, 'You don't live in Germany'.

At the centre of this scene is a highly poetic description which crystallizes Arthur's deranged picture of the cruelty and folly of the world. It complements the visual imagery of the play with a corresponding force and precision of verbal metaphor:

D'you dream? – So do I. D'you dream about the mill? There are men and women and children and cattle and birds and horses pushing a mill. They're grinding other people and cattle and children: they push each other in. Some fall in. It grinds their bones, you see. The ones pushing the wheels, even the animals, look up at the horizon. They stumble. Their feet get caught up in the rags and dressings that slip down from their wounds. They go round and round. At the end they go very fast. They shout. Half of them run in their sleep. Some are trampled on. They're sure they're reaching the horizon . . . Later I come back. There's a dust storm. White powder everywhere. I find the mill and it's stopped. The last man died half in. One of the wooden arms dropped off, and there's a body under it. (*Plays One*, p. 185).

It is worth pointing out that Bond has pre-empted any over-emotive delivery of this speech by his rigorous provision throughout of objects – here George's skull, elsewhere the Doctor and Len's corpse – which oblige the actor not to internalise the speech, whitewashing it with an emotional colouring of his own feelings, but to externalise it and thus present the poetic images in stark outline. The tug-of-war on Beachy Head translates Arthur's idea into a savagely comic visual reality which terminates the scenes on earth.

It was the imagery of the scenes set in heaven together with the sexual metaphors relating particularly to Florence Nightingale which originally gave cause for the strongest objections to the play. When we examine the presentation of Florence we realize that metaphor is indeed the correct term to describe the manner in which Bond conveys her changing role in the play. The development of Florence is almost as significant as that of Arthur, and it is in no way related to conventional concepts of character portrayal. Bond's manipulation of this historical figure is the most original and imaginative feature of the play, one very easy to misinterpret in reading. At the beginning of scene 5 Florence comes on stage and says:

I'm changed. Queen Victoria raped me. I never dreamed that would happen. George will know. I'll disgust him . . . I've started to have evil thoughts. Her legs are covered in black shiny hairs.' (*Plays: One*, p. 155)

We should not be misled by the stage direction '*distraught*' which prefaces this into thinking there is any attempt here to present a naturalistic reaction to rape. Rather Bond is alerting us to the intensity of Florence's change. The rape is of her mind and ideas, the sexual reference a metaphor for the corrupting force of Victorian ethics. The further elaboration of this in the scene with Mennings and the conversations with Victoria are indications that her innocence has been destroyed. Bond does not attempt to dramatise the rape on stage – as Howard Brenton does in *The Romans in Britain*, also to convey a political message through a physical image – and his restraint allows him greater flexibility in handling Florence's subsequent metamorphoses.

She is a truly Protean figure, changing to convey different shifts of meaning. The full consequences of her indoctrination are seen in her position as first hangwoman in history, her devotion to the troops – in which Bond shows her innocence prostituted in the cause of war – and her final death. When she arrives in Heaven she narrates vividly how she died:

> O, after the catastrophe I had to earn my living. (VICTORIA clicks her tongue). I opened a brothel, and business was so brisk I didn't have time to get up. I catered for ministers, probation officers, WVS hierarchy, women police chiefs – Well, there I was, in bed with Disraeli and Gladstone. They always shared a booking. They got very excited as usual and just then Gladys (a nom d'amour) said 'Listen'. There was a newsboy shouting in the street. Mafeking had been relieved. That on top of the rest was too much. They got over-excited – and here I am. (*Plays: One*, p. 201)

This has all the sharpness and satirical force of a political cartoon, Gillray's celebrated picture of Napoleon and Pitt carving up the world, for example. It conveys with economy and wit the fact that, in lending her support to a corrupt system, Florence has in the end been sacrificed: screwed by opposing political interests.

Images of cannibalism develop throughout the drama. At first – in the trial scene – they are restricted to descriptions as Len and Joyce dispassionately relate the killing and eating of the man who jumped the cinema queue. It is significant that Bond should have called his heartless young criminal by the same name as the hero of *Saved*, since the social realities of the earlier drama are projected into the political context of *Early Morning*. That he is a different character is made clear from Albert's initial description 'Oddly enough Arthur was talking about him. He said he'd murder his mother for five shillings if he hadn't already done it for the experience'. Albert's linking of Len and Arthur here anticipates the later action as Arthur tries to understand the motives behind Len's conduct. He will get no sense from Len who turns on him with the assertion 'I got a right to be guilty same as you'. Len is wholly vicious, the cannibalism treated in such a matter-of-fact manner in the trial being a symptom of a sick culture, like the titles of the films – 'Policeman in Black Nylons' and 'Buried Alive on Hampstead Heath' – over which he and Joyce quibble. Arthur will have to look beyond psychological motives to discover the reason for Len's conduct. He will discover it in the madness and corruption of the society of which he is a member – an insanity which finds the literal counterpart of its ethic in heaven, as he discovers on his arrival there:

ALBERT. In heaven we eat each other.
VICTORIA. It doesn't hurt.

ALBERT. And it grows again.

GEORGE. Like crabs.

VICTORIA. Nothing has any consequences here – so there's no pain. Think of it, no pain. Pain is just a habit. You forget all your habits here. Bon appetit. (*Plays:One*. p. 200)

This play also represents Bond's most extensive employment of a device characteristic of his drama as a whole: anachronism. It is a form of *Verfremdungseffekt*: a method of shifting perspective suddenly which is at the same time witty. Albert's comments to Disraeli at the beginning of scene 4 are the first example of this technique in the play:

It must look as if some stray fanatic kills her. We just step in to keep the peace. We close the ports and airfields, take over the power stations, broadcast light classics and declare martial law. (*Plays: One* p. 147)

In a flash the relevance of the historical action to the present is indicated. It is in this very scene that the device is most fully used as Victoria presides over the trial of Len and Joyce. Here the anachromism serves to show the extent to which our own society is judged and ordered by an outmoded irrational set of values. Gradually we see the Victorian and the modern world brought into closer contact as we are made aware of the way in which our own culture is dependent on and influenced by a perniciously irrelevent ethic. Bond's play could be defined as surreal in that by juxtaposing images from different periods and contexts he forces us to appreciate a dislocation between what we observe and what we are taught to believe. This artistic technique is a precise one; it gives sharp definition to the viewpoint he explains in the Preface to *Saved*:

There will always be some people sophisticated enough to do the mental gymnastics needed to reconcile science and religion. But the mass of people will never be able to do this, and as we live in an industrial society they will be educated in the scientific tradition. This means that in future religion will never be more than the opium of the intellectuals. (*Plays: One*, p. 312)

Linked to the dramatic device of anachronism is that of parody. With Bond, moreover, the latter takes on the implications of the musical meaning of the term: as sustained imitation, rather than mere satiric deflation. This is particularly the case with the two trial scenes: the first on earth, the second in heaven. In the former the whole judicial procedure is mocked from the start. Victoria's first request – to Florence – is 'Pass me that hat dear, I'm sitting in a draft', and after Florence has handed her the black hanging cap she puts it on and comments: 'Black's my lucky colour'. The trial is a travesty of justice, even though the accused are more guilty than even Victoria imagines since she is unaware Len has agreed to murder her. It is precisely the same situation as occurs in *The White Devil* where Vittoria can object: 'You have ravish'd justice': she has been convicted in a sham trial but her accusers do not appreciate the extent of her crimes. The trial in heaven is a parody of that on earth. Bond's topsy-turvy logic is inexorable. All the guilty parties from earth – from Len to Victoria – are present in this monstrous inversion of the afterlife which is organised on precisely the same criteria as the world. Therefore in this court where 'the father prosecutes and the mother defends' it is necessary to be proven guilty to be admitted to heaven. In this parody of the Last Judgement witnesses are produced who vie with one another to convict Arthur with a mounting catologue of accusations:

He kills
He's a nose picker.
He looks at dirty pictures.
He picks his nose while he looks at dirty pictures.
He kills.
He can't control his natural functions.
He's only got unnatural functions.
He kills.
He eats dirt.
He is dirt.
He dreams about killing.
They ought to name a venereal disease after him.

(*Plays: One*, p. 198)

Bond's parody is at its most imaginative in the presentation of Florence. When Len is taken to Victoria to inform
her of the whereabouts of her sons, Florence is disguised as
John Brown, an impersonation she finds increasingly
difficult to sustain in the later scenes because as she says, 'I
can't do the accent.' There is a hilarious farcical moment
when George is brought back to life, sees Florence and
demands why she is wearing a moustache and strange
clothes. Florence tells him she's in fancy dress and Victoria,
never slow at improvising reasons and excuses, adds:
'We're going to a party. To raise money for war wounded.'
Not all Bond's satiric techniques carry an equal weight of
significance: the John Brown impersonation is an inspired
piece of comedy which gives the play added speed and zest.
The parody of Florence as The Lady With The Lamp is
even funnier, but more savage both in its iconoclasm and
the implications of this: that her kindness in support of war
can only be misplaced. She is not an angel but a whore,
serving the interests of a predatory state. The scene is set
not at Scutari but at Slough, and the soldiers further link the

Crimean war to more recent history with their litany: 'Bless yer mum. God bless yer mum. Angel a Mons. Angel a mercy. Underneath the lamp light dum di dum di dum'. This is the most shocking, most offensive scene in the play with the obscene ribaldries of the soldiers complemented by Florence giving herself to the winner of the raffle, Ned, whom she describes as 'the purest person I know. He has most of the virtues of Christ, and none of his vices.'

The treatment of Gladstone is equally unreverential. Bond cunningly does not reveal his identity until we have seen him as a bully supervising the beating up of Len according to the rule-book. We also learn later in the scene that Len is his son, a further shock which brings home to us a brutal oppression on the part of the right-wing trade union leader which is a match for the unscrupulousness of his political opponents. A brief but telling scene of literary parody is that in which Arthur meets his father's ghost who urges him to revenge his death. The *Hamlet* reference is clinched by George's deranged impressions, first of a cockerel and then of bells, in an attempt to make the ghost think dawn is breaking and that he must return to his grave. Albert is here tempting Arthur with a recourse to violence. He is as dangerous as the Ghost of the gravedigger's Boy in *Lear*: a plea to return to the conduct and ethics of the dead past rather than to work out in the present a revolutionary course of action for the future.

The plot, the central images, the anachronisms and the parodies have an economy and wit which are matched by the verbal dexterity of the text. Bond complained to me that critics had originally objected to his portrayal of Victoria as unfair. 'I didn't think I'd been unfair', he commented, 'I made her intelligent and witty when she was in fact a very stupid woman – and a murderess to boot.' She is always in command of the situation, never at a loss for words, as in her conversation to the officer in charge of the firing squad at Bagshot:

> VICTORIA: Splendid turnout. How's Mrs Smith?
> OFFICER: Mrs Jones, ma'am?
> VICTORIA: I thought so, Major Jones.
> OFFICER: Captain ma'am.
> VICTORIA: Nonsense, I've just promoted you. I have a favour to ask in return. Shoot them both. (*Plays: One*, p. 180)

When the squad, on counter-orders, point their rifles at her instead, she comments imperiously: 'Let me warn you: I fire the last shot', and when Disraeli then arrives she snaps: 'Private Jones, you're cashiered.' Bond reserves his funniest joke for the moment later in this scene when Disraeli is shot and Gladstone enters, whereupon Victoria pronounces: 'We are not amused.' This quick-witted repartee is matched by the Lord Chamberlain's epigrammatic style which permits Bond to satirize official and reactionary views, as in the opening of scene 3 when he comments to Mennings:

> I'm as modern as anyone, but I'm all for holding trials in secret and executions in public. That simplifies government and satisfies the people. We should never have abolished hanging. It was something to live up to. (*Plays One*: p. 143)

Bond is fully aware of the relationship between social position, moral viewpoint and witty style. In *The Sea* and *Restoration* he takes his analysis further and at the same time provides a counterpart and opposition to the assurance of his more articulate characters by giving new expressiveness to the language of their adversaries.

Once again Bond's strongest weapon in the play is paradox, and once more there is an intriguing parallel with Shaw. The comic verbal paradoxes of the play culminate in the extensive inversion of traditional values in heaven. In *Man and Superman* Don Juan discusses the afterlife with Ana:

DON JUAN. Do you suppose heaven is like earth, where people persuade themselves that what is done can be undone by repentance; that what is spoken can be unspoken by withdrawing it? That what is true can be annihilated by a general agreement to give it the lie? No: heaven is the home of the masters of reality: that is why I am going thither.

ANA. Thank you: I am going to heaven for happiness. I have had quite enough of reality on earth.

JUAN. Then you must stay here; for hell is the home of the unreal and of the seekers for happiness. It is the only refuge from heaven, which is, as I tell you, the home of the masters of reality, and from earth, which is the home of the slaves of reality. (*Man and Superman*. p. 99)

Like Shaw, Bond reverses the traditional Victorian picture of heaven and hell; but for him heaven is not better than earth, but worse. He contradicts conventional religious assumptions by reproducing and magnifying here the madness of the world. Hence the place is intolerable for Arthur, whilst the rest of the family, as well as Len and Joyce, are perfectly happy, as unaware as they were on earth of the hell of their lives. His father's prophecy has come true: Albert's ghost had told him: 'the living haunt the dead. You will learn that.' Arthur explains this paradox to Florence in their crucial scene together:

ARTHUR. Most people die before they reach their teens.
Most die when they're still babies or little children. A
few reach fourteen or fifteen. Hardly anyone lives on
into their twenties.

FLORENCE. Thank God.

ARTHUR. Bodies are supposed to die and souls go on
living. That's not true. Souls die first and bodies live.
They wander round like ghosts, they bump into each
other, haunt each other. That's another reason why
it's better to die and come here – there must be peace
when you're dead. Only I'm not dead. (*Plays: One*, p.
209)

What Arthur has come to realise is this: Society destroys
man's will and spirit, dehumanising people, as we see in the
case of Pam's family in *Saved* or Len and Joyce in this play.
Human beings become little better than zombies if they are
not nurtured on a vital culture. Arthur is different. He has,
like Len in *Saved*, seen people at their worst and has
learned to make a stand against the brutality and conformi-
ty enforced on him. His stand, too, is a small one: he refuses
to eat. Thus he remains stubbornly alive and will – in the
final scene – literally transcend this environment. As he
goes on to explain to Florence:

'I've tried but I can't die! Even eating didn't kill me.
There's something I *can't* kill – and they can't kill it for
me. Pity – it must be nice to be dead. Still, if I can't die I
must live. I'm resigned to my curse! I accept it. I'll
probably even end up being happy. (*Plays: One*. p. 210)

This speech is the nub of the play. As with Arthur's
desperate remedy which is analysed at length in scene 11 –
the hectic pace of the action is halted again whilst Arthur

thinks through his dilemma. Here he lays down the foundations for a new life, having observed the contradictions of the old in all their clarity. At this point it is too much for Florence who cries out: 'Let me alone! You're a ghost! Ghost! Ghost! You're haunting me – O stop it!', but by the end of the scene, though confused, she can say: 'Perhaps I'm alive, perhaps we needn't be like this. I'm trying to think'. Her reactions precisely parallel those Bond wishes to provoke in the audience. We may at first be puzzled and offended by the situation he presents through paradox, but, though we may initially reject what he is saying, it is possible that later – perhaps months later – we may come to understand and accept the truth of his presentation. We find ourselves in the same position as Florence at the end of the play, sitting apart, trying to come to terms with a challenge which is capable of radically changing our lives.

'The Sea'

The Sea, Bond's most complete exercise in tragicomedy, is a very different play from either *Saved* or *Early Morning*. It is set in 1907 in a small East Coast town and shows the attempt of the central character Willy to come to terms with the death of his friend Colin who has been drowned. The play is important in Bond's development as the clearest statement he makes on the necessity to come to terms with tragedy, to see things as they really are and to go on living. The emphasis in this drama is very strongly on the personal. Though the characters are seen in a specific social context at a particular historical point in time. *The Sea* is the least overtly political of Bond's plays. Willie is an outsider: he does not belong to this society, and it is his encounters with the three principal figures – Mrs Rafi, Hatch and Evens – all three of them eccentrics, which enable him to understand more fully his own position. Compared with *Saved* and *Early Morning*, *The Sea* is a very static play. Very little happens: the tragic event – Colin's death – occurs off stage in the opening scene; thereafter we are presented with a sequence of scenes dramatising small-town life. Aspects of this are notably bizarre: Hatch's tearing up of the velvet and his attack on Colin's corpse, as well as Mrs Rafi's amateur dramatics, both in her rehearsal of the Orpheus play and at the funeral. But all these features are closely related to the play's social environment and the corresponding pressures it creates on the characters.

The Sea was written straight after *Lear* and immediately before *Bingo*. The Shakespearian allusions are significant, particularly within the context of tragicomedy. After *Lear* Bond felt the need to compose something at the furthest remove from its catalogue of violence and horror. There is perhaps an irony in the fact that whilst in *Bingo* he was to go on to present Shakespeare at the end of his career as a disillusioned suicide, thereby negating the message of hope vested in the images of rebirth and reconciliation in the last Romances, his own sequel is this gentle life-enhancing drama which has a number of close affinities with *The Tempest*. The parallel is firmly established in the opening scene with its powerful stage directions:

> *BEACH.*
> *Empty stage. Darkness and thunder. Wind roars, crashes and screams over the water. Masses of water swell up, rattle and churn and crash back into the sea. Gravel and sand grind slowly. The earth trembles. (Plays: Two* p. 105)

Willy, like Ferdinand, must suffer and learn. He must face

reality: Colin will not be re-born and the future for him and Rose is a very far cry from Miranda's 'brave new world', as the final lines of the play reveal:

> ROSE. I followed you. We mustn't miss our train. What were you saying?
> WILLY. I came to say goodbye, and I'm glad you – (*Plays: Two* p. 169)

Bond ends on a question mark here because Willy must now reconcile the advice given to him by the old hermit, Evens, with what he has seen in the conduct of Mrs Rafi and Hatch. Mrs Rafi's Orpheus drama – a play within a play – is fraught with more problems than Prospero encounters in presenting his masque for the benefit of the young lovers, whilst Mrs Rafi's attempt to stage-manage Colin's funeral misfires as spectacularly as Prospero's wedding celebration. It is Evens, the wise old seer – quoting from the Chinese poet Li Po – imparting his knowledge to Willy who more completely fulfils the function of the magus Prospero. In the final scene of the play he obliges Willy to observe the condition of the world with such a depth of rational analysis that the young man is encouraged to build on the foundations of his philosophical propositions.

Everything in the drama is tending towards this final confrontation. Unlike Arthur in *Early Morning*, however, Willy is a more silent observer, still recovering from the emotional blow of his drowned friend. It is Evens who is the more articulate thinker, expounding here an evolutionary argument which – once again – has strong affinities with Shavian philosophy. Evens's credo begins with a statement recalling Orwell's *1984* – 'I believe in the rat. What's the worst thing you can imagine?' – but this drama so concerned with predictions for the future will transform

Orwell's symbol of horror into a positive emblem. Evens continues:

> I believe in the rat because he has the seeds of the rat-catcher in him. I believe in the rat-catcher. I believe in sand and stone and water because the wind stirs them into a dirty sea and it gives birth to living things. The universe lives. It teems with life. Men take themselves to be very strong and cunning. But who can kill space or time or dust? They destroy everything but they only make the materials of life. All destruction is finally petty and in the end life laughs at death. (*Plays: Two* pp. 167-8)

This is very close to the central thesis put into the mouth of Don Juan in *Man and Superman*: the strongest expression of Shaw's faith in an evolutionary future. Elsewhere in his plays Bond's evolutionary emphasis tends to be more firmly political; here is its complement in a more abstract philosophical explanation. It is Evens too who explains – in his first meeting with Willy – the meaning of tragedy:

> It's always the details that make the tragedy. Not anything larger. They used to say tragedy purified, helped you let go. Now it only embarrasses. (*Plays Two* p. 118)

It is a sense of perspective, of not being lost in the individual heart-breaking incidents which represent the destructive side of life, that informs Bond's consistent ethic. From the dogged determination of Len in *Saved* through to the enlightened revolutionary action of Wang in *The Bundle* or Hecuba in *The Woman* there is a vision which looks beyond tragedy. *The Sea* is the last of Bond's plays to express an alternative essentially in the format of tragicomedy; after this he has attempted more and more to confront tragedy not so much with comedy as with an epic structure to give added strength to his emphasis on political issues.

Whilst Evens encourages Willy to hope: 'The truth's waiting for you, it's very patient and you'll find it', he also presents a picture of humanity at its worst in a nightmare image of the future:

> When your life's over everything will be changed or have started to change. Our brains won't be big enough. They'll plug into bigger brains. They'll get rid of this body. It's too liable to get ill and break. They'll transplant the essential things into a better container. An unbreakable glass bottle on steel stilts. Men will look at each other's viscera as they pass in the street (*Plays: Two*, p. 168)

This envisages mankind entirely stripped of its humanity: a world 'without grass' and 'without tragedy' where 'there's only discipline and madness'. The implications of such a world are glimpsed already in the play through the attitude and conduct of Mrs Rafi and Hatch. The latter, a victim of the society presided over by Mrs Rafi, is a figure who elicits complex sympathies. He is bullied and put upon, a slave to the whims of his autocratic and privileged customers. But he is a chilling example of petit bourgeois vindictiveness, taking out his sense of social inferiority in a manic extension of racism. This crazed little draper envisaging an invasion from outer space is for all the world like a caricatured version of H.G. Wells whose own description of the Martians in *The War of the Worlds* was precisely of 'unbreakable glass bottle(s) on steel stilts.' The violence in this drama is confined to Hatch: his attacks on the velvet, Mrs Rafi and Colin's corpse are risible, a particularly ironic note being struck in his conviction that he has killed an alien when Colin's corpse oozes water instead of blood. But the violence, handled here in a markedly different theatrical style from *Saved* or *Early Morning*, is no less firmly related to social and political realities. Hatch is a pathetic victim of his class, just as Mrs Rafi is trapped by her own bourgeois indoctrination. It is only the outsider, Evens, who – like the hermit, in *The Pope's Wedding* – is able to teach Willy a valuable alternative.

In Mrs Rafi there is an attempt to organise society according to an ethic which is essentially Victorian. Mrs Rafi's attempt to bring discipline into her life is the last stand of a nineteenth century authoritarian faced with a new society and a new century. Victoria died in 1901; the play is set in 1907. As with his picture of Victoria, Bond's presentation of Mrs Rafi is richly comic and this old harridan is also endowed with a much stronger depth of sympathy, notably in her lengthy final speech to Willy which counterbalances the propositions of Evens. Here she sees the futility of her life with a clarity and honesty that is at the same time endearing through its wry humour:

MRS RAFI. I'm afraid of getting old. I've always been a forceful woman. I was brought up to be. People expect my class to shout at them. Bully them. They're disappointed if you don't. It gives them something to gossip about in their bars. When they turn you into an eccentric, it's their form of admiration. Sometimes I think I'm like a lighthouse in their world. I give them a sense of order and security. My glares mark out a channel to the safe harbour.' (*Plays: Two*, p. 160)

There is more than a touch of Shaw's Mrs Warren here: that 'aimiable old blackguard of a woman' defending her way of life. Bond fully exploits the technique Shaw admired and copied from Ibsen, of leading from exposition through development to discussion, in Willy's confrontation first with Mrs Rafi and then with Evens at the end of the play. But Mrs Rafi asks herself the same question Shakespeare will ask at the end of *Bingo* and reaches the same conclusion: 'Has anything been worthwhile? No, I've thrown my life away'. Bond also employs a particular style of comedy in his presentation of Mrs Rafi to bring home more clearly and precisely the social implications of his critique of her world. She is modelled firmly on Wilde's Lady Bracknell, no-where more clearly than in her dictatorial handling of Hollarcut:

> MRS RAFI. You can come and work *hard* in my garden every evening for the next two months. There's a lot of especially *hard* digging you can do. That, or I must take up this matter with the local magistrate. Which?
> HOLLARCUT. (*grumbling*) Diggin', I suppose.
> MRS RAFI. I'm glad you've got some wits left. I shall assume Hatch led you astray – an easy assumption. Present yourself at my back door tomorrow at five-thirty sharp.
> HOLLARCUT. Mornin' or evenin'?
> MRS RAFI. Both.
>
> (*Plays: Two*, p. 160)

But Mrs Rafi's class is a doomed one, as she recognises in her inability to hold her society together by force. Her own failure is a microcosm of the situation Bond has presented in *Early Morning*, handled here with a very different theatrical style but entirely consistent in its viewpoint. When Willy later teases Hollarcut over his enforced labour he receives the cryptic response: I'll tell you something you ought to know, boy. I dig for her (*He lays the side of his index finger against the side of his nose and looks crafty.*) – but will anything grow? . . . Mornin'. It is a mark of Bond's immense versatility as a comic dramatist that here he can present his continuing critique of society with a warmth and humanity which is at the furthest extreme from the grim realism of *Saved* or the outrageous satiric savagery of *Early Morning*.

5
Epic Theatre:
Dramatising the Analysis

All art aspires to the lyrical, just as truth tends to the simple.
And in epic the lyric becomes objective. The artist tries to
show reason in experience and appearance – and lyric is the
daily appearance, the commonplace dress of reason. It shows
us the rational. It makes the epic pattern human. It's the
footprint on the pathway. In the epic-lyric the individual and
the particular are no longer isolated but are placed in a
historical, social, human pattern.

The Activists Papers, p. 131.

We have examined in previous chapters how Bond's
experiments with dramatic form have resulted in an
undermining of conventional responses to the theatrical
medium and in a rejection of tragedy and its implications.
In the first instance essentially classical and bourgeois
theatre forms have been made to yield a powerful subversive potential; in the second a variation of tragicomedy has
been effected which looks beyond the social, ethical and

political iniquities of the present to a more optimistic future. These two contrasted styles are complementary in that they both challenge the status quo and demand new patterns of thought, more rational methods of organising society. There is a third area of Bond's work which is more radical: it presents an even more savage picture of abuse and irrationality and in turn suggests more precise answers to the problems dramatised.

Bond said that in a trio of plays: *Bingo*, *The Fool* and *The Woman* he had been concerned with 'the burden of the past which makes change so difficult' and went on to state:

> I'm now going on to a series of plays which I will call 'Answer plays' in which I would like to say: I have stated the problems as clearly as I can – now let's try and look at what answers are applicable (Hay & Roberts p. 266)

The first of these 'answer' plays was *The Bundle*, a re-write of *Narrow Road To The Deep North* and a drama as harsh and uncompromising as the earlier play had been witty and straightforward. Yet *Narrow Road* ends in despair: with the onstage suicide of Kiro, whilst *The Bundle* shows us a picture – though not wholly idyllic – of the post-revolutionary state. Two other plays since *The Bundle* have dramatised revolution: *The Worlds* which is concerned with 'cold' revolution; with strike action and terrorism, neither of which prove effective, and *Human Cannon*, which deals with the activities of a group of revolutionaries during the Spanish Civil War. There is a pronounced development through these three dramas in that *The Bundle* does not show how the revolution is achieved whilst *The Worlds* contrasts the tactics of two different pressure groups threatening the status quo and *Human Cannon* reveals the

difficulties of initiating and achieving effective revolutionary conduct.

Bond's most recent plays have firm roots in his earlier
drama. The latest works have a close affinity with *Lear*.
Here too is a piece about revolution which is written in a
style quite unlike any of Bond's previous dramas. It has a
vast scope, as its reference to Shakespeare's tragedy
implies, and a matching cast: over eighty speaking parts,
played in the first production by a group of twenty three
actors. *Lear* was Bond's first epic play. Its theme is
essentially political; it concerns the evolution of society and
the heavy compromises that are made in forging a new
state. It is the first of Bond's plays to have links with the
Greek epics through this theme, whilst it has obvious
affinities with Elizabethan and Jacobean theatre in its
presentational style. It is also the first of Bond's plays to beg
the comparison with Brecht in its subject matter and
dramatic technique, both of which have much in common
with the German dramatist's own definition and practice of
Epic theatre.

Dramatists do not always care for detailed analyses of
their indebtedness to the techniques of previous craftsmen
and it would be misleading to see Bond as any conscious or
deliberate pupil of Brecht. Brecht is an artist Bond admires
– more, in fact now than at the time of writing *Lear* when, as
he has since pointed out, his knowledge was limited by the
small number of Brecht's plays in translation and his
inability at that time to read German. His attitude has
changed over the last fifteen years so that the dramatist he
could refer to as a creater of 'naive melodramas' in 1971 he
now sees as 'the most important writer of his era'. (Both
phrases are taken from articles in *Theatre Quarterly*, Vol II
no. 5 p. 13 and Vol III no. 30 p. 34 respectively). The latter

quotation is from Bond's reply to an article by Peter Holland which draws extensive parallels between the work of the two writers. Holland argues that the early policy of the Royal Court and the work of William Gaskill in particular aroused Bond's interest in the techniques of Brecht and that in most of his dramas – notably *Saved*, *The Sea* and *The Fool* – the influence of Brecht makes itself felt essentially in a concern with the social bases of behaviour and an attempt to deny conventional causality to a sequence of events. In his reply Bond pointed out that he had been influenced more directly by the visit of the Berliner Ensemble to London in 1956 than by the work at the Court shortly after this and made his own position in relation to Brecht very clear:

> Brecht was an experimenter, an explorer. He did not answer all our questions. The time between his death and the present has given us more experience, more history to draw on. The tragedy of twentieth century drama is that Brecht died before he could complete a last series of plays: the plays he would have written as a member and worker of a Marxist society. The loss is very severe. But we have to write the plays he left unwritten. (*Theatre Quarterly* No. 30 p. 34)

Holland's article was unfortunately timed. It was written before any of the plays from *The Bundle* onwards had been performed. Yet it is odd that the one earlier play that bears such striking resemblence in scope and method to Brecht's work – *Lear* – should be the only one he does not discuss. It is important in our exploration of Bond's epic dramas that we are aware from the start of a shared outlook on the part of the two writers which inevitably results in the deployment of similar theatrical strategies. Bond has not taken any of these directly from Brecht; his political intentions in the later epic dramas are more extreme and if we observe similarities of method we must also realise that Bond inevitably goes further than Brecht in disturbing and challenging his audience. In recognising affinities with Brecht then, we are dealing with a different situation from that which obtains in those plays – such as *The Woman* or *Restoration* – where Bond has consciously chosen to emulate a dramatic model for his own purposes. The parallels here are those which exist between two Marxist writers developing the political potential of epic theatre at different points in time.

In 'A note To Young Writers' included in *The Activists Papers* Bond states:

> The form of the new drama will be epic . . the essence of epic theatre is the way it selects, connects and judges. Even when it deals with two people quarelling in a kitchen it draws its method and values from the understanding of the history of all men. How else should you judge between right and wrong? . . . the broad structure of history must be understood before the incidents in it can be given meaning. (*The Worlds* p. 108)

'Theatre', Bond argues, 'must talk of the causes of human misery and the sources of human strength'; what he demands is a 'rational theatre'. Such a theatre is epic precisely because it sees beyond individual psychological issues to social and political truths. It is epic in the Aristotelian sense as distinct from dramatic in that its focus is wider. Such a theatre is realistic, as Brecht explained:

> The crux of the matter is that true realism has to do more than just make reality recognisable in the theatre. One

has to be able to see through it too. One has to be able to see the laws that decide how the processes of life develop. These laws can't be spotted by the camera. Nor can they be spotted if the audience only borrows its heart from one of the characters involved. (*Messingkauf Dialogues*: p. 27)

It was Brecht who went on to explain the crucial 'shift of Accent' which further determines the technique of epic as distinct from dramatic theatre. In the notes to *Mahagonny* he points out that whereas dramatic theatre thrives on plot which implicates the spectator in a stage situation and wears down his power of action, epic theatre is concerned with narrative, turning the spectator into an observer and arousing his power of action. In dramatic theatre the human being, taken for granted, is unalterable, whereas in epic he is the object of the enquiry and able to alter. In terms of the play's structure, dramatic theatre forces the spectator's eyes on the finish since the scenes build from one to the next in a process of growth, whereas in epic theatre the audience have their eyes on the course where each scene works for itself in a process of montage. Bond inevitably shares this attitude, though he has challenged the final implications of Brecht's theory in requiring a more complex interdependence of scenes:

It's true that each scene must stand for itself as an aspect of the whole. But there must also be a cause and effect relationship between the scenes. This is necessary because life is ordered by cause and effect, incident and choice, problem and decision and this reality must be reflected in the structure of the play. (*Theatre Quarterly* No. 30 p. 35)

The 'cause and effect' in Bond's later epic plays is not the psychological development of bourgeois drama; it is a process by which characters are forced to make choices, often difficult ones because the ethics of the situation are complex and paradoxical. It is precisely in observing this necessity to choose wisely, to decide the right way out of a problem that Bond continues the tactic he employed in *Saved* by throwing the ultimate responsibility on the audience. It is we who must revalue, must reassess our situation. Bond's attitude is identical to that of Brecht's Philosopher in the *Messingkauf Dialogues* who rejects the neatness and inevitability of conventional dramatic theatre:

> You see, I've got another passion besides curiosity. That's disputatiousness. I like carefully weighing the pros and cons of everything I see and putting my own oar in. There's a certain pleasurable doubt in me. I finger people's acts and utterances just like a poor man fingering his loose change, and turn them over ten times. And I don't think you people here leave elbow room for this doubt of mine; that's what it is. (*Messingkauf* p. 18)

Anyone who has conversed with Bond will recognise his affinity with Brecht's delightfully ironic self-portrait.

Though Bond undoubtedly did not 'get his Brechtianism from the Court' as he asserts in his response to Peter Holland, he was fortunate to discover in William Gaskill the ideal interpreter of his earlier plays there. Gaskill had explored techniques of Brechtian acting in much the same thoroughgoing way that Brook and Marowitz had experimented with Theatre of Cruelty effects in their season at Lamda in 1963. In the previous year Gaskill had directed a much praised production of *The Caucasian Chalk Circle* at the Aldwych Theatre, which was generally agreed to be the first fully successful attempt to translate Brechtian theory into practice in this country. In an interview published in *Encore* Gaskill described some of the acting exercises he had employed in rehearsing this production. They are significant for two reasons. Firstly, they give a clear indication of the type of preparation necessary for plays in the epic mould and thus illustrate the bases of his success in directing Bond's drama; and secondly they provided the technical groundwork on which Bond himself has built as a theatre practitioner, both in his capacity as a dramatist, and, later, as a director of his own plays.

Faced with the problem of how to start rehearsing with actors more accustomed to a Stanislavskian tradition, Gaskill hit on a telling example. He asked for a cigarette and when one of the actresses gave him one he asked the company why she had done so. A series of responses followed, all based on emotional or psychological reasoning. Gaskill went on to stress to the company the significance of the social gesture and to point out that if such a scene were played so as to convey merely generosity on the part of the actress or scrounging on the part of the director it would lack truth. From this he went on to improvise a series of scenes around the theme of giving and taking a cigarette in which the actors related what was going to happen in the improvisation *before* actually doing it. The presentation of the scene then followed plus a discussion of how accurate a demonstration the narrative had been. Gaskill's conclusions are important in our consideration of Bond's epic drama:

> You will find that though (the actor) will *state* the narrative clearly, he will often present it emotionally,

and in fact what he is presenting *is* the emotion. Soon he gets the hang of it, and it does teach him more than anything else, a peculiar awareness. This awareness is the important thing. It doesn't matter what he wants to do in the scene, provided he sees what it *is* that he is doing. Most actors – certainly English actors – tend to present everything at once, a bit of emotion, a bit of character, a bit of social content, throwing it all at you in a great muddle. And this exercise is designed simply to make the actor think clearly. Now in Brecht the actor is never there to present the emotional situation, he is there only to present the unbiased narrative. That is, the actor had to state the narrative in its simplest and most economic form, cutting out anything that was not absolutely necessary. (*Theatre At Work* p. 126)

Particularly telling is a further account by Gaskill of how two of the actors explored the murderers' scene in *Richard III*. It was only when they came to realise that the two men are habitual murderers who are paid to kill that the full sense of the scene emerged. Previously they had seen the characters as 'a sadist and a coward come to murder the Duke of Clarence', but – comments Gaskill –

When they played it on the basis that these were two habitual murderers, so that the one who was frightened wasn't really all that frightened because he had committed murder before, and the sadistic one was sadistic but he was also doing the job for money, then the scene worked. (*ibid*. p. 127)

Bond too encourages a duality of response in his actors so as to define more precisely the inter-relation of social and psychological motivation basic to their conduct.

Edward Bond

'Lear'

Lear is a play about revolution. It is also a play about violence. Though the two themes are complementary they are not synonymous, and it may be that the excessive amount of realistic physical violence in this play – far greater than in any of Bond's previous dramas and never equalled in any play since – considerably alienated reviewers and public alike when the play was first performed. A more recent production (1983) directed by Barry Kyle for the Royal Shakespeare Company met with a much greater measure of success both in England and abroad, the production being successfully toured on the Continent. Whilst he admired the playing of Bob Peck as Lear, Bond deplored the decision in the production to add musical sound effects at all the violent climatic moments. He complained that they gave the production some of the spurious thrill of a Hollywood film. *Lear* is not a melodrama and any addition of music in this vein could only serve to blunt the play's attack. Perhaps for this reason this revival proved more palatable than the original production.

There is, however, a problem with the amount of violence in the play. In the Preface Bond himself stated:

> I write about violence as naturally as Jane Austen wrote about manners. Violence shapes and obsesses our society and if we do not stop being violent we have no future. People who do not want writers to write about violence want to stop them writing about us and our time. It would be immoral not to write about violence. (*Plays Two*: p. 3)

This is Bond in characteristically aggressive, paradoxical vein, answering those critics such as the Lord Chamberlain or Pamela Handsford Johnson who had previously attempted to silence him as a writer. A problem, however, arises as a result of the particular nature of the violent scenes presented. We are plunged into a scene of savagery at the start of the play. Lear executes a worker for causing the death of another man building his defensive wall. Even his daughters think this unneccessary and cruel; it appears the more so as the man's death is delayed by the interruptions to Lear and the consequent suspense and tension built up in the audience. This is the first of many 'aggro effects' as Bond calls them in the play. He explained the necessity for them in his reply to Peter Holland's article:

> Alienation is vulnerable to the audience's decision about it. Sometimes it is necessary to emotionally commit the audience – which is why I have aggro-effects. Without this the V- effect can deteriorate into an aesthetic style. Brecht then becomes 'our Brecht' in the same sloppy patriotic way that Shakespeare becomes 'our Shakespeare'. I've seen good German audiences in the stalls chewing their chocolates in time to Brecht's music – and they were most certainly not seeing the world in a new way.' (*Theatre Quarterly* 30, p. 34)

We should look more closely at the concept of 'Verfremdung' as outlined and practiced by Brecht as well as the way in which it is handled by Bond.

Brecht's celebrated 'V effect' was a method of alerting the audience to a different perspective: he cites the example of a schoolmaster suddenly losing his dignity and threatening aspect when seen pursued by the bailifs. A striking example in his drama is the conversion of the ludicrous figure of the vegetable dealer into the strutting ranting figure of the Führer in *The Resistible Rise of Arturo*

Ui. In the celebrated English production with Leonard Rossiter in 1968 it was the scene with the ham actor which most strikingly established this shift of perspective. In a production I witnessed at the Schauspielhaus in Hamburg in 1976, however, the full implications of this conversion were reserved until the very last scene. Throughout the play the parallels with Hitler – though clear enough – were not over emphasised. In the final scene, however, the actor gave a complete impersonation of the Führer as the set transformed itself in an exact replica of the panoply of a Nuremberg rally. The effect on the audience was the exact opposite of that described by Bond above: a riot broke out in the auditorium with protests against this representation of painful history being shouted down by cries of 'Nazi raus!' The debate went on into the street and well into the night. It is surely the response Brecht intended when he warned:

> Neither the public nor the actor must be stopped from taking part emotionally; the representation of emotions must not be hampered, nor must the actor's use of emotions be frustrated. Only one out of the many possible sources of emotion needs to be left unused, or at least treated as a subsidiary source – empathy.' (*Messingkauf Dialogues* p. 57)

Brecht expressly stated that 'any effort to present scenes and characters so that they can be *bloodlessly noted and weighed up* would be quite unneccessary and even harmful for our purpose' (*ibid* p. 54, my italics.)

Bond's attitude is very similar. His 'aggro effects' are most in evidence in the torturing of Warrington, the rape of Cordelia and death of the Gravedigger's boy, the blinding of Lear and the 'anatomising of Regan' – a grimly ironic physicalisation of the Shakespearian original. All these scenes are profoundly disturbing; they are meant to be so, as is the stoning of the baby in *Saved*, the first and perhaps still the most emotionally upsetting scene Bond has ever created. But the violent scene in *Saved* is the representation of the consequences of a deeply engrained violence in society and its institutions. It is intended to make the audience consider the far greater obscenity perpetrated by the political establishment. The violent scenes in *Lear* – and there are many more of them – function in a somewhat different way. They are more direct representations of the cruelty of oppressive regimes. And whilst there is irony in these scenes it is more inescapably savage. The violence of Lear's own regime is exceeded by that of Bodice and Fontanelle who are responsible for the torturing of Warrington and the attack of the soldiers which leads to the rape of Cordelia and the death of the Gravedigger's boy. But even these atrocities are matched by the systematic blinding of Lear, a political act, totally without sadistic motive and carried out with clinical efficiency, which reflects the added ruthlessness of Cordelia's revolutionary regime.

The challenge – or problem – for the theatregoer is two-fold. There is an escalating violence in the play which makes very tough demands on an audience; and there is no apparent escape from it: each society outdoes the oppressiveness of the previous one. Bond's condemnation of totalitarianism is unsparing; the hope for a revolutionary utopia is unfounded, as Lear makes plain to Cordelia:

> Listen Cordelia. If a god had made the world, might would always be right, that would be so wise, we'd be spared so much suffering. But we made the world – out of our smallness and weakness. Our lives are awkward

and fragile and we have only one thing to keep us sane: pity, and the man without pity is mad. (*Plays Two* p. 98)

It is the same conclusion Arthur reached after having passed through madness in *Early Morning*. Moreover there is a further parallel with this earlier play. The agent of proletarian totalitarianism in *Early Morning* is Gladstone, revealed as an insensitive right-wing trade-union bully. Bond does not identify this figure of working-class aggression until he has been revealed in his worst colours. Only then does he introduce himself.

In *Lear* the identity of the young woman who undergoes the extremes of suffering in Act I is not named until the final climactic moment when her husband, having emerged from the well, sees what is happening to her and twice calls her name; 'Cordelia!' before being shot. There is a fundamental alienation effect here akin to that associated with the identification of such a famous historical figure as Gladstone. We are jolted by this recognition, surprised that this woman – not one of Lear's daughters – is Cordelia. She will be hardened through her suffering and when she confronts Lear in Act III Bond springs another 'Verfrem dungseffekt'. Now the tearful figure of Act I has turned into the tough guerrilla fighter who refuses to compromise. She never liked Lear but her rejection of the truth of his humanist plea is the more savage as we are forced to adjust to her new-found strength, a strength which denies basic human needs.

The climactic scene of Act I is a fine example of another feature of epic theatre: Gestus. Brecht's plays convey the essence of their meaning in powerful stage images. The concept of gestic acting and performances implies a combination of the implications of the words 'gesture' and 'gist' in English: a concentration of visual meaning. The stage picture in Bond's drama is always precise; not a detail is wasted; there is no room for extraneous action or movement. He is a writer who conceives of his ideas not essentially in words but in images. The accumulated tensions of Act I – tensions generated by the social and political events of the drama rather than by psychological or emotional issues – culminate in the scene presented so vividly in the Stage Directions as the BOY emerges from the well:

> SOLDIER E shoots him. He staggers upstage towards the sheets. His head is down. He clutches a sheet and pulls it from the line. CORDELIA stands behind it. Her head is down and she covers her face with her hands. SOLDIER D is preparing to rape her. The BOY turns slowly away and as he does so the sheet folds round him. For a second he stands in silence with the white sheet draped round him. Only his head is seen. It is pushed back in shock and his eyes and mouth are open. He stands rigid. Suddenly a huge red stain spreads on the sheet. (*Plays Two*. pp. 43-4)

This is an 'aggro-effect' expressed through the precision of a complex Gestus. The image is complex because it reflects not only the violence of the immediate events as a heritage of accumulated aggression, but points forward to the different roles which both Cordelia and the Boy – who will return as a ghost to haunt Lear – will afterwards assume.

Another feature which Bond's epic style shares with Brecht is its humour. Though the events of *Lear* are grim in the extreme a savage ironic humour pervades the play. It is most in evidence in the torturing of Warrington, Act I scene 4. Here Bond skilfully contrasts the attitudes of the two sisters to the conduct of the soldier who is mutilating the captured general. Bodice is calm, unruffled, continuing with her knitting and passing disparaging remarks on the conduct of her sister. As Fontanelle helps the soldier to jump on Warrington's hands, shrieking 'I want to sit on his lungs! Bodice remarks wrily: 'Plain, pearl, plain. She was just the same at school.' This comment is made directly to the audience and is intended to provoke laughter. Our response is therefore complex: the emotional effect of the scene is disturbing but our empathy is prevented by the comments of Bodice who comes between us and the action. It is rather like a more aggressive version of the scene in Shakespeare's play when our intuitive sympathy for Lear in the hovel is modified by the ironic comments of two other 'madmen', the professional Fool and Edgar, the counterfeit 'Bedlam beggar.' The history of epic theatrical writing in England provides us with further examples of the way in which an ironic perspective can be utilised to provoke a more complex response to violence. In the Wakefield 'Buffetting' play in the Towneley medieval miracle cycle the conduct of Ananias and Ciaphas is contrasted, the former coolly insisting they proceed by law, the latter allowing himself to be carried away in a sadistic frenzy of hatred. In *The Duchess of Malfi* Webster sets the shrewd pragmatism of the Cardinal against the passionate intensity of his brother, Ferdinand, in their consideration of how to deal with their sister who has defied them by secretly marrying.

Such a juxtaposition of opposing attitudes to violence generates a more complex response in an audience. In the scene in *Lear* we are forced to evaluate the nature of the violence and understand the horror more deeply. We are not allowed the relatively comfortable experience of emotional catharsis nor allowed to reject the cruelty. The laughter Bodice elicits from us both makes us accomplices and yet shocks us into a more considered response. Bond has gone very much further than Brecht in his stage techniques here, but there is a similarity of approach in that the latter insisted on the virtues of 'Spass' (fun) and 'Leichtigkeit' (lightness of touch) in the presentation of horrific acts on stage, praising the acting of his company in *Fear and Misery in the Third Reich* thus:

> But what was so unusual was that the players never performed these ghastly episodes in such a way that the spectators were tempted to call out 'Stop!' The spectators didn't seem in any way to share the horror of those on the stage, and as a result there was repeated laughter among the audience without doing any damage to the profoundly serious character of the performance. (*Messingkauf Dialogues*, p. 72)

Lear dramatises the overthrow of an oppressive regime by a revolution which itself develops its own rigorous ethic. The arbitrary cruelty of Lear is carried further in the indiscriminate savagery perpetrated by his daughters when they seize power; but the new order led by Cordelia soon establishes a more efficient system of terror which suppresses all opposition or criticism. Bond has said that:

> Act One shows a world dominated by myth. Act Two shows the clash between myth and reality, between superstitious men and the autonomous world. Act Three shows a resolution of this in the world we prove real by dying in it. (*Plays Two*, p. 12)

This statement comes at the end of a long introduction devoted to the more important theme of the work: the violence bred by oppression. As with *Saved* and *Early*

Morning the final gesture of defiance against a mad destructive society seems at first a very small one: Lear climbs to the top of the wall – the wall he had built and which Cordelia maintains as a defensive strategy – and begins to dig into it as he is shot. Lear, like Len and Arthur, has learned a great deal and he has attempted to convey his knowledge to others. But he is an old man; he learns very late. We must wait for other revolutionary heroes; Wang in *The Bundle* and Agustina in *Human Cannon* – to achieve more effective action because it stems from greater knowledge born through long experience.

In *Lear* Bond might at first appear critical of revolution. He is critical rather of the conduct of those who are insufficiently educated in the needs of society that they mistakenly replace one form of tyranny with another.

I don't see Lear's last act as futile. If measured in quantitative terms – then yes, it's just a few spadefulls of earth. But he has turned the whole myth round, that is what is important. He tells the girl to go back and describe to the others what he's done. In other words he is making a teaching gesture. That's all I needed to do in this play, otherwise, like Schiller in *St. Joan*, I idealise the theme. The play was a preparation for what would follow. I needed to distance myself from Stalinism because that was a propaganda-block to socialism in the West. Having done that I could go on to argue for the revolution. I made Cordelia the daughter of a priest because Stalin was trained as a seminarist. I think that even with Stalinism socialism is better than capitalism because capitalism degenerates into fascism. Given (though I hope I never am) the choice, I'd choose Stalinism: the argument is gone into by Agustina and her husband in *Human Cannon*. (Letter to the author: 4.8.84)

In his later epics he examines in far more detail the ethics of revolution and in so doing answers questions which have their origins specifically in *Lear*.

'The Bundle'

The subtitle of this play is '*New Narrow Road To The Deep North*': it develops themes from the earlier drama as well as returning to the subject-matter of *Lear*. *The Bundle* is a play about revolution but it differs from the two earlier works both in its positive emphasis and in its discovery of radical new theatrical techniques to present this shift of focus. It opens, like *Narrow Road*, with a scene in which the poet, Basho, discovers an abandoned child and leaves to pursue his own personal search for enlightenment. In the earlier play the child grows up to be the tyrant, Shogo; in *The Bundle* the revolutionary hero, Wang. *Narrow Road* then goes on to dramatise the conflict between different repressive regimes – a frequent theme of the earlier plays – contrasting Shogo's tyranny with the methods of the imperialist Europeans, the Commodore and Georgina.

Bond calls the play 'a comedy' and there are strong links with *Early Morning*, notably in the farcical juxtaposition of values (here Eastern and Western) and the parody of the Victorian ethic. The two come together in Georgina's explanation of her methods to a bemused Basho:

> GEORGINA: Shogo ruled by atrocity . . . It didn't work because it left people free to judge him . . . instead of atrocity I use morality. I persuade people – in their hearts – that they are sin, and that they have evil thoughts, and that they're greedy and violent and destructive, and – more than anything else – that their bodies must be hidden, and that sex is nasty and

corrupting and must be secret. When they believe all that they do what they're told. They don't judge you – they feel guilty themselves and accept that you have the right to judge them. (*Plays: Two*, p. 208).

Again there is an echo of Shaw, of Tanner in the first scene of *Man and Superman* who opposes Ramsden's hypocrisy with the argument:

We live in an atmosphere of shame. We are ashamed of everything that is real about us; ashamed of ourselves, of our relatives, of our incomes, of our accents, of our opinions, of our experience, just as we are ashamed of our naked skins . . . The more things a man is ashamed of the more respectable he is. (*Man and Superman* p. 14)

Narrow Road is essentially satiric, the ironies culminating in the overthrow of both regimes, the disillusionment of Basho and the suicide of Kiro, too wrapped up in his own self-indulgent despair to notice the man who almost drowns because he does not help him. In returning to this subject Bond creates a very different, much tougher drama. Only Basho remains from the original and he is treated far more critically, whilst the satiric contrasts of the earlier play are translated into the thought provoking ironic juxtapositions of *The Bundle*.

Bond is also returning more significantly to the theme of Georgina's speech but developing this into a more complex analysis of the relationship between personal and social morality. The *Note on Dramatic Method* which prefaces the play is a vital new pointer to Bond's change of emphasis in this play, explaining his heightened awareness of the artist's function and method. It is the playwright's duty – argues Bond here – 'to re–write human consciousness', to resolve the discrepancies between pragmatic social reality and outmoded ethical values, to replace political and moral hypocrisy with a valid workable scheme of values. The successful repression imposed by Georgina is based on a superimposition of alien moral values: 'when they believe all that', she points out, 'they do what they're told.'

Modern society, argues Bond, functions in much the same way:

> Social institutions control the tacitly accepted view (of the world) by means of education, the selection of information, economic sanctions and if necessary naked force. Above all they control the tacitly accepted *moral* code – and social living requires a moral code (or a reactionary substitute for it) as well as a set of rules.

But:

> our social institutions do not represent the interests of those people who by experience as workers and consumers are creating developments in human consciousness, new ways of understanding and interpreting the world, and so making necessary new ways of organizing it. (Preface to *The Bundle*, pp. vii-viii)

The artist's task is thus straightforward but uncompromising. Bond sees theatre as uniquely capable of validating 'human standards, ways of living, ethical decisions, understanding' precisely because it proceeds by 'demonstrating the relation of cause and effect in practical human life and not merely in concept or theory.'

One of the consequences of Bond's sharper awareness of the responsibility of the dramatist in his most recent plays has been the search for a valid new dramatic and narrative

form. His sensitivity to contrasted models of theatrical structure – from Restoration mannered comedy to Greek tragedy – has as its corollary the desire to create valid new methods of telling a story. Unlike the Absurdists who abandoned plot in their total negation of conventional aesthetic and ethical values, Bond – a highly skilled story-teller – knows that this craft is basic to the way his dramas function. Yet he is aware, because of the dislocation between institutionalised morality and the real working world, that dramatic narrative can all too easily be misinterpreted:

> As we cannot merely tell stories or record events we have to handle punctured myths or broken stories. Effect no longer follow cause, judgment no longer assesses deed, as they did in the past. Not even imagery works for us as it did in the past. Above all moral language is caught in the same trap. So it is not easy for contemporary writers to contain experience and moral teaching in myths and stories in the way a more secure settled society could. (*ibid* pp. xiv-xv).

The consequence of this approach is two-fold: it results in a rejection or reworking of myth, as in *Lear* or *The Woman*, and a revaluation of the techniques of the dramatist who most fully set himself the task of recording the events of contemporary history: Brecht.

The 'Note on Dramatic Method' moves therefore from an assessment of the social and political challenges facing the dramatist to a specific examination of the particular methods employed by Brecht to present his own stories. Bond sees the value of interrupting a scene with placards explaining what is going on and commenting. Apart from the new perspective offered there is the thrill of observing that tragic inevitability can give way to an awareness of the ability to alter events: that the rise of Arturo Ui, horrific in its consequences, was nevertheless '*resistible*'. But, argues Bond, 'there is a limit to what this can achieve. It merely says that something is so and, even though it is in fact true, saying it does not test or prove it in the laboratory of art, in the rationality of the stage' (ibid p. xvii). A similar criticism applies to the technique of caricature. Bond is in total agreement with Brecht in seeing a character not so much as an individual as a class function, but he believes it is necessary to guard against simplification. If the difference between social and ethical positions is not recorded from reality the play's moral statements may not have been tested and proved but merely assumed: 'The analysis of an event must not swamp the recording of it. We have to show the mask under the face not the mask on it.' (ibid p. xvii). As a final comment on Brecht's distinction – in the Notes to *Mahagonny* – between the concept of montage basic to epic and the process of growth intrinsic to drama Bond argues that the idea of 'every scene for itself' is dangerous since this isolation of scenes does not accurately present reality. The playwright, Bond emphasises, 'should dramatise not the story but the analysis' and it is the analysis which dictates the structure of the story. Bond feels there is a weakness in *The Caucasian Chalk Circle* in that Azdak, though showing us that in theory judgment can be wise, disappears before he can illustrate the practicality of this. Bond concludes:

> Practicality can only be shown by the ordering of scenes, not by incidents in scenes. The epic's structure must have meaning – it is not a collection of scenes showing that meaning is logically possible. The epic must have a unity based on practical truth, just as once it was based

on mythological coherence. This unity comes from the analysis, which demonstrates, embodies cause and effect in a coherent way. (*ibid* p. xx).

The story of *The Bundle* is in some respects even simpler than that of *Narrow Road*; the complexity resides in the telling of it, in the arrangement of incidents which represents the dramatisation of the analysis. In the first scene Basho abandons the baby; it is, however, rescued by a poor ferryman and brought up as his son. Wang, the child, raised amidst the extreme poverty of his society, makes a series of crucial decisions which are instrumental in initiating revolutionary action. Unable to offer money or goods to save his parents from the flood, Wang sells himself as a slave instead. After serving his nine years as slave to Basho, Wang himself comes upon an abandoned child. He kills it rather than increase his own economic dependence as his step-father had done. Meeting up with a group of robbers he becomes their leader, educating them from briggandry to revolution. In the second part of the play a wider commitment to revolution is expressed. Wang's step-father is persuaded to assist his son in smuggling guns to the rebels and subsequently to sacrifice his own life to protect Wang. Wang, with painful restraint, refuses to assist an oppressed woman until the gesture is productive of useful revolutionary action. When he learns the Landowner is leaving in a hurry he realizes the time has come. The rebels take over and establish their own more just society.

Bond points out in the introduction that the play is best understood not 'as a story of Hero Wang' – heroics are out of place in this context – but 'as a demonstration of how the words 'good' and 'bad', and moral concepts in general, work in society and how they ought to work if men are to live rationally with their technology, with nature and with one another.' (*ibid* p. xviii). The ethical viewpoint is identical to that taken in *Saved* – Bond is deeply critical of outmoded, hypocritical, irrational moral standards – but now the paradoxes of the earlier play have been converted into pointed juxtapositions and comparisons which force the audience to evaluate more precisely the rights and wrongs in an unjust society. The most striking example of this technique is the parallel between the end of scene one and the end of scene four. In both a man has to decide whether or not to sacrifice himself and others in saving an abandoned child. In the first scene the ferryman is torn between compassion and reason; such an intuitively kind action is economically irrational; he and his wife will suffer. Bond dramatises this pull of values in clear physical terms as the Ferryman looks at the child, stops, goes to the child, gets into the boat and poles away, stops rowing, poles back to the child and finally picks it up. The two points at which he stops are punctuated by the cry of a curlew, a call for natural compassion. He gives in to this, saying wryly: 'We must be hard to live. Yet at any moment a curlew can call and we are lost.' (*The Bundle* p. 4) In scene four Wang is faced with the same dilemma but his response finally is different. After a scene with the child's mother which heightens the emotional tone of the action, Wang, recognising this child is but one of many abandoned and demanding help, answers:

WANG No!
> *As he hurls the child far out in the river he holds a*
> *corner of the white sheet in his hand and it unravels,*
> *catches the wind and falls to hang from his Hand.*
> The world is shivering – there! Who will speak? (*The*
> *Bundle* p. 29).

As with the simple actions of rowing and halting in the first scene, so here the physicalisation of Wang's difficult decision is concentrated into a powerful gestic image. This epic technique, an inheritance from Brecht, has further affinities with the German playwright since Bond is concerned here, as was Brecht – most notably in *The Caucasian Chalk Circle* and *The Good Woman of Setzuan* – with the difficulty of doing good. Grusha rescues a child and brings it up as her own; later the decision as to who is the true mother will be argued out. In order to control her destructively sympathetic impulses Shen Te is compelled to invent the harsher personality of Shui Ta to protect herself. Brecht's theme is the impossibility of making clear moral decisions when the society in which you are living is itself iniquitous. Bond objects to the lack of practicality in Brecht's resolution of the problem in *The Caucasian Chalk Circle*; he might just as well have criticised the literal use of a *deus ex machina* (or rather the *three* gods) which interferes in the affairs of Shen Te. The final line of *The Good Woman of Setzuan* is Shen Te's 'Help!' Bond is concerned to make that cry resound much more painfully in his audience's minds. The destruction of the child by Wang is unexpected and shocking, the more so as he himself has been rescued from a similar predicament. But the sort of moral blackmail implied here is invalid; more significant is the wider moral issue – that by losing yourself in individual emotional situations you neglect the more important objective: how such a situation can be changed.

This technique – disputatiousness, to employ Brecht's term, dramatising the analysis according to Bond – is most powerfully in evidence in the scene later when Wang once again refuses to act compassionately. This is in scene seven when he is faced with the cruel punishment of the woman who has been forced to wear a huge stone cangue round her neck as punishment for stealing cabbage leaves to make broth. The injustice of the situation is obvious but Wang cannot act impulsively as Tiger wishes to do. He knows the woman and wishes above all to help her; but instead he bites the inside of his lip to stop shouting out. The visual image on stage focusses the complexity of the emotional and moral issue which is, by contrast, expounded clearly and rationally:

WANG. (*there is a sudden fall of blood from WANG'S mouth. As he talks it runs down his chin*). No. The ox bears the yoke. Break the yoke. Another yoke is put on its neck. The farmer has fifty yokes in his store. Stop being an ox. What is the use of breaking a window when it has iron bars? The landowner still controls. When he needs soldiers he sends – and they come. So people fear him. If we're kind to the woman – he must be crueller to the people. So they say: 'She deserves to be punished.' They act out of fear. That is their morality. The only morality they can have. Learn it: the government makes not only laws, but a morality, a way of life, what people are in their very nature. We have not earned the right to be kind. I say it with blood in my mouth. When the landowner is no longer feared then our kindness will move mountains. That is our morality, Tiger. Today we should look on kindness with suspicion. Here only the evil can afford to do good. (*The Bundle* p. 54)

Again an extension of Brechtian theatrical technique is observable here. There is a parallel with scene three of *Mother Courage* when Courage is obliged to fake lack of concern in not recognising the body of her dead son. But the suppression of emotion in this scene from *The Bundle* rivets our attention on the complexity of the moral analysis whereas in Brecht's play the incident serves rather as a cruel irony at the climax of an independent scene.

Bond further stimulates debate by the placing of the above scene in the second half of the play. It occurs between the two scenes dramatising the commitment of Wang's father to the revolutionary cause and, again, because it serves to interrupt the story, makes us more aware of the difficult choice forced on him. Instrumental in focussing the conversion and in involving the audience in the decision-making process is the handling of the bowl of water by the Ferryman here. Bond states that the water-bowl is first an object in the story and 'then it is abstracted from the story and put into the analysis' (p. xviii). This occurs as the Ferryman presents his decision to the audience:

FERRYMAN. (*simply and calmly, as if he no longer had to struggle with his thoughts but knew what to say. He holds the water in front of him. Close to his chest.*) Why are our lives wasted? We have minds to see how we suffer. Why don't we use them to change the world? A god would wipe us off the board with a cloud: a mistake. But as there is only ourselves shouldn't we change our lives so we don't suffer? Or at least suffer only in changing them? (*Noiselessly, carefully he puts down the bowl*) (p. 64)

The detailed stage directions to the Ferryman at this point are the result of Bond facing and resolving a difficult problem which arose in rehearsal. Bob Peck, who played the Ferryman in the first production, was tending to treat the situation as a personal problem and to act in a naturalistic style. Bond has commented:

Bob was thinking of his son (who might be killed next) and was mumbling away to himself like Willy Loman – and the bowl was something a sad old man was fidgeting with. Watching all this was one of the reasons why I knew I had to direct my own plays so that I could make things clearer and understand the actor's problems more. (Letter to the author: 4.8.84)

Benefitting from the work with Bond on the scene, Bob Peck was able to explain how this episode – a prime example of what the playwright was subsequently to define as 'public soliloquy' – functions:

> I have learned that the Ferryman's first question has to be pushed out directly to the audience. Doing that integrates it with the bowl image. If the audience isn't included directly in that first question, the effect is lost when I put the bowl down at the end of the speech. If I have included them, when the bowl finally goes down it's as if it is offering it to them and saying: "Look – this is what we are doing." The image is integrated into the speech. (Hay and Roberts p. 284).

As Bond has put it: he 'offers the audience an elucidation, just as earlier he had offered Tiger the clear water.' It is the visual clarity with which complex ethical issues are presented that gives Bond's later epic dramas their force and originality.

'The Worlds'

Of all Bond's plays to date *The Worlds* most thoroughly dramatises analysis as distinct from reinterpreting myth or presenting and commenting on action. The title page of the rehearsal script alludes to a speech from *Timon of Athens* (Act IV scene 3) which had obsessed Bond when he was previously working on *Bingo*. It is Timon's diatribe against the corrupting power of gold which in *The Worlds* relates to the capitalist ethic in general and to Trench's relationship to it in particular. There is a further parallel with the Shakespearian companion piece, *King Lear*, in Trench's rejection (like Timon's) by his business friends and his self-imposed exile from their world. This comes about after the kidnapping of Trench by a group of terrorists who promise to return him only if Trench's company accede to their striking employees' demand for a wage increase. The terrorists' attempt misfires and Trench, back at the firm, discovers his managerial colleagues have profited from his absence to demote him as chairman and put the company on the stock exchange. Like Timon, he invites them all to a party at which he insults them and then goes off to live in the abandoned house where he had previously been held prisoner by the terrorists. A second attempt by the terrorists fails as they capture the chauffeur in mistake for the new chairman. Finally they are betrayed and captured whilst Trench shoots the chauffeur.

Like *The Bundle* this play has a straightforward plot; everything depends on the construction and arrangement of the scenes which are designed to open up and question the ethical issues. There are in fact four worlds in this play and it is the inter-action between them which is productive of a complex analysis of society. In an interview Bond discussed the ethics of these different cultures in detail. Of Trench he commented:

I'd like him to be played a bit like Samuel Beckett. He represents that sort of liberal culture which is like the

Bloomsbury group who were all the time being rude about the generals and the blimps who were in fact paying them and keeping their homes for them. Once the connection between the two gets broken then that culture becomes deeply reactionary because it is not a real culture. Bloomsbury is an incipient form of reaction. It takes very little to waltz from that to blackshirts. (Interview with the author: 9th June 84)

'The route Trench takes', Bond added, 'leads to a philosophy of despair, of seeing no meaning in life, of destruction.' Hence he finally murders the chauffeur. The business world of which Trench is at first a part is the 'slick, ruthless, ganster world of international business; a really vicious world'. Bond comments:

> What happened in the past is that the Bloomsbury culture – the élite culture – could form some alliance with this business world, emblandish it, so that its destructive powers were hidden. That relationship has now collapsed and it is out of that collapse that you get oppositional groups: the terrorists and the strikers. (*ibid*)

Though Bond is presenting the inter-relation here of two cultures he deeply despises: the Absurd ethos of the pessimistic liberal and the cut-throat ruthlessness of the capitalist, he does not present them in a simplistic caricatured way. It may seem from the first scene with its parody of the glib heartiness of business colleagues that his aim is deflationary and satiric, but the complacent banalities and the self-congratulation give way in the next meeting to a presentation of what Bond has termed 'the mask under the face, not the mask on it.' Reality is very much more ruthless and dangerous than the first scene might imply. Trench's colleagues soon take advantage of his absence, precisely manipulating the threats of the terrorist kidnappers to their own ends. Later, after the second kidnapping attempt they are seen in an even more sinister light. Not only are they quite happy to pay the hundred thousand pounds demanded, as it is expedient for their public image to appear compassionate, but in the scene which follows Terry, through his ironic analysis of what the chauffeur is worth: 'A Workman's Biography', underlines precisely how such a worker is manipulated and treated by his bosses:

> Hundred thousand pounds? Waitin in drafty corners. Sitting outside nightclubs till three in the morning. Ain done his health no good. Say ninety thousand. Gettin on. Eyesight's goin. Bad hearing. Has to ask 'where to' twice. Say eighty thousand. Wife not too good. Needs nursin. Can't manage the late nights. Seventy thousand. Mrs Kendal wants something younger so she can score off the other rich slags. And she'd like to pull into a lay-by on the way home. Which is bad when you're getting on. Fifty thousand. Votes Tory to please the boss. Thirty thousand. Lives in two pokey rooms cause the rent's controlled. No central heatin. Stairs bad for his heart. Twenty thousand. Reads the *Sun*. Ten thousand. Never double crossed a customer. Never put one over on the public. Five thousand, Nerves going. Kendal bawls him out in the hold ups for not drivin out on top of the other traffic. One thousand. On tablets to get himself started in the mornins. Very dodgy. Bloody hell – we owe you! (*The Worlds* p. 72)

It might be objected that here Bond is giving his working class character far too much insight and too subtle a control of irony for someone in his situation. But here we have an example of what Bond has discussed in the 'Activists Papers' which accompany the printed text of the play as a 'public soliloquy.' Bond is particularly concerned that socialist writers do not patronise the working class by simplifying their outlook on life. It is vital that political playwrights put three-dimensional characters on the stage and not what Bond has called 'schematized class functions.' An equivalent must be found for the psychologically rounded character, the figure who is sufficiently complex to be able to surprise us and yet who has an observable consistency of behaviour. Bond is not interested primarily in matters of psychology, however. As he says in the poem 'Advice to Actors':

> Actors
> Don't try to make your character possible
> Men do things that ought not to be possible
> Don't say 'he'd never do this'
> Men don't behave in expected ways
> Don't make the character one man
> Unfortunately a man is many men
> Don't worry when an action isn't consistent
> Men aren't consistent
> Ask why they're not consistent

The impression of complexity in Bond's characters which makes them compelling and interesting comes not from a presentation of their multifaceted personalities, but from an observation of the ways in which they react in specific social situations.

In moments of hightened insight when a character, responding to his circumstances, sees beyond the immediate situation he deepens his self-awareness by intensifying his consciousness of his own position and that of others in society. When Bond chooses to open the situation in this way it can go further than the example cited above. We observe an extension of the technique employed in *Restoration* whereby the working people are endowed throughout with a broader perspective of history expressed through their songs. In Part II scene 3 Terry is given what Bond names in the script 'a public soliloquy' in which he transcends the immediate circumstances – the boardroom and the negotiations between management and strikers – with a vision of how a socialist society would organize matters more rationally and efficiently. Bond explains and defends such a dramatic technique thus:

> What the character says must still be right for his character. His subjective individuality then helps to explain the truth of his objective, generalized statements: in the future these things will be because there are *now* people like him. So it would be nearer the truth to say that the author becomes the spokesman of his character. The actor doesn't step out of character but the audience sees the character's potential self, sees him as he could be. (*The Activists Papers* p. 140)

Bond also points out that such a technique of public soliloquy need not be confined to specific moments in the play.

He also points out that 'a large part, perhaps all of Scene four (Part One) could be acted as a group public soliloquy.' This is another powerfully gestic scene in which Terry – the most aware of all the workers – explains and illustrates how oppression works and how the morality of violence makes the police agents with management against the workers. Acting out a brief charade Terry steals Beryl's purse and shows how he is caught by the police. This simplistic morality gives way to a more complex situation in which John plays Trench who steals three pounds from Terry claiming this is his profit. When Terry wishes to get one back he is obliged to strike ('bein law abidin') and then finds the police are not interested in the working man regaining his stolen money. 'Trench relies on force as much as any terrorist', is Terry's point, driven home by John's comment: 'Yeh! The terrorists have caught Trench at his own game.' This debate – like the soliloquy of Part Two Scene Three – is made public in order to draw the sceptical Ray and thus the audience into the dramatisation of an analysis which, when the interaction of all four worlds is considered, is highly complex.

Bond's sense of irony gives the issues dramatised in this play a resonance and richness which avoid the dangerous extremes of myth and polemic. His sympathies are more obviously with the strikers and the terrorists, though neither group is presented without criticism and full awareness of the contradictions inherent in their situation. In his new Author's Note to *Plays: One* he challenged conventional liberal attitudes to violence by stating:

If you decide never to use violence you have still done nothing to make the world less violent. That can only be done by making it more just. I am not a pacifist, we have to say what things are and not what we would like them to be. Reason is not yet always effective, and we are still at a stage when to create a rational society we may sometimes have to use irrational means. Right-wing political violence cannot be justified because it always serves irrationality; but left-wing political violence is justified when it helps to create a more rational society, and when that help cannot be given in a pacific form.

(op. cit. p. 16-17)

This is a carefully thought-out position, one matched in the play which, whilst it gives the most rational statements to Anna, the terrorist, nevertheless sees them distorted entirely by Trench in his reading of the ultimatum, a reduction of the ideas to syntactical nonsense which parallels the way the media and Trench's class misrepresent such attitudes. But Anna and her accomplices are compromised more fully by the betrayal of their group as well as by their own impractical folly in kidnapping the chauffeur in mistake for the boss. In a sense, however, the terrorists are more effectively betrayed by the workers who should support them and who are far from unanimous in their approach. In Part Two Scene Four Terry confronts Ray who is prepared to go back to work and offends the older man by his hard-line stand. His own attitude – expounded most completely in the 'Workman's Biography' – is the more ironic since, whilst he is insisting on the chauffeur's status as a cheap commodity in the eyes of the management, his own friend John is attempting to sell him an over-priced motorbike. Such a neat irony is reflected in the wider scope of the play; as Bond has amusingly commented:

> Now what happens is that the marriage between Trench (Bloomsbury, or the Absurd, if you like) and the business side is split up by divorce rather dramatically, whilst the marriage between the terrorists and the strikers is not consummated. (Interview with author 9th June 1984)

Bond does not refuse to answer the questions he has raised in the play. He is more concerned to present an analysis of the way in which our society functions, our worlds interact so as to give his audience valuable materials with which they may examine and reconstruct their lives.

6
The Way Forward

I believe still that we have to learn to dramatise the analysis –
which means getting closer to reality than myth ever could.
What I hanker for is what Lessing suggested: that poetry
should be a creation of 'natural signs' so that the dramatised
analysis could become a new form of story which would be
open to a demythologised human consciousness. That would
be a story outside ideology: and would be of practical working
use to the hearers – not so much as an explanation of the
inexplicable in their lives – or a rationalisation of the repressed
and exploited lives they live – but a practical tool of consciousness for people who were in control of their lives: really people
who owned themselves. That's also what I mean when I say
that literature always aspires to the lyric. There aren't any
'natural signs' in Lessing's sense. Language is political and only
becomes transparent when political understanding replaces
ideology. Then the language we speak isn't internally working
against us. But I can imagine a free society where language
could function as if it were a natural sign, because human
beings understood their situation. Till then, we can make
language speak directly by combining it with truer images –
that is what political theatre is concerned with. (Letter to the
author 21.6.84)

Bond is an iconoclast: for him the writer's task is to destroy an ideology which society mistakenly reverences. Yet he is equally concerned to replace this with a rationally organised ethical and political structure. His plays have been concerned with attacking or demystifying figures as different as Queen Victoria and Shakespeare in order to expose the inheritance of moral guilt and hypocrisy associated with the former and to question the role of the artist in society through his dramatisation of the latter. These represent the two most extreme examples of historical characters who have been subjected to his particular brand of ironic perspective. He is no less sparing of atrophied conventions and out-dated institutions: the judiciary and the church are presented in a highly critical light throughout his work. The army is never presented with a shred of sympathy in his plays; it represents the most brutal and barbarous form of ignorance and oppression. War and the pity expressed for the fallen by poets such as Owen and Sassoon inspire him with anger. In a poem called *First World War Poets* he complains:

> You went to the front like sheep
> And bleated at the pity of it
> In academies that smell of abattoirs
> Your poems are still studied.

To some Bond seems pitiless and insensitive; an aggressive attacker of establishment figures and conventions. Yet he is the most constructive of writers. His aim is to make us aware of false gods, of unworthy ideals, of irrational circumstances. The above poem continues:

> What did you fight for?
> A new world?

No – an old world already in ruins!
Your children?
Millions of children died
Because you fought for your enemies
And not against them! (*The Bundle* p. 85-6)

The attack on respected figures – morally and aesthetically held in the highest esteem – is merely the cover for a more subtle tactic: the method of confronting us with a moral choice and making us question the hallowed approach to this subject. We should learn to know our real enemies, Bond insists; they are the pillars of that society millions of troops died to protect. He employs similiar devices throughout his plays to disarm conventional attitudes and make us question the neatness of our ethical assumptions. From a Shavian use of paradox, through an exploration of the subversive potential of established dramatic forms, he has developed to a unique brand of epic theatre which is structured so as to dramatise the analysis of these ethical issues within a clearly defined social and political context.

Bond will use whatever theatrical tools are available to chip away at encrusted beliefs and topple unjustly revered images. He has worked and will continue to work in every possible venue: from the large public forum of the Olivier stage through to the clubs and fringe theatres visited by the newer smaller groups of theatrical artists who share his beliefs. But whether directing the nation's most esteemed actors or young inexperienced students his criteria on performance are fixed and consistent with his political beliefs. He is radically opposed to the mystique of acting. For him drama has no sub-text, no secret meaning which it is the actor's special skill to unearth and present. He requires the actor to relate part of the character he is playing to his own personality, but what is more important is his awareness of the external world. In place of the aesthetic emphasis on the mystery of the artist's inspiration and the actor's calling, he substitutes an insistence on craft and skill which observes the complexity of the character's view of life and position in society. He is not concerned with the hidden inner life of his stage figures but with their routes of communication with others, an emphasis which replaces in-depth psychology with historical and social perspective, thus giving the character and the drama a new richness of texture.

His awareness of the actor's skills and how to train them has deepened with his own commitment to directing his plays. He has invented and developed exercises precisely aimed at enabling the actor to extend his sympathy with the character into a fuller awareness of his social and political circumstances. One such exercise is that of the burning house. Bond encourages his actors to react to the fact their child is trapped in a burning house and asks them to attempt to persuade the others to help them. At first the actors pull out every emotional stop, use every trick in an attempt to win sympathy. Bond then asks them to repeat their improvisation but assuming a specific profession. This not only serves to control their excessive emotionalising, but forces them to ground their appeal in observable social reality and thus make their case more effectively. It is a precise image of the way Bond's polemical theatre works, an extension of Brechtian stage technique into a passionate but controlled command of language.

Unlike Beckett, for example, Bond is a writer who does not have a set idea of how his plays are to be done. He mistrusts the sort of actor who brings to the role certain assumptions of his own and applies them to the character. The actor who refuses to believe that his character is capable of certain acts, insisting he knows how such a person would behave, is as irresponsible and dangerous as the person who turns a blind eye to political realities. Bond believes that 'good' and 'evil' are labels which are of no use to us anymore. They must be broken down and questioned. This applies equally to the function of acting. Another technique Bond has refined in encouraging such an open-ended attitude in both performance and audience is the playing of a potentially tragic scene as farce. There is a fine example of this in *Derek* when the mother, entirely overwhelmed by the sudden wealth her son has brought home, throws the money out of the window and thus causes him to be arrested. The whole speech in which she narrates this is punctuated with explosions of uncontrollable laughter, Bond's aim being to show the character whipped from tragedy to farce as we are made aware of the enormous waste of her ability that has made her the nagging and destructive woman she now is. At the end of *Summer* Bond writes another scene of farce as Xenia returns to find the flowers whilst David learns that his mother is dying. Bond insisted that Anna Massey make the most of the flowers as a prop from farce and provoke the audience to laughter by her exaggerated reactions to them. In this way both the actor and the audience are unable to resolve the problem of the play neatly and are encouraged instead to understand the issues more fully and allow this awareness to influence their own lives.

This refusal to provide neat or all-embracing solutions is at the root of Bond's mistrust of directors. A director can distort a play more completely than an actor, as this description of the final scene between Arthur and Florence in Peter Stein's production of *Early Morning* makes plain:

The happiness of these two is a direct product of their hopelessness, of the knowledge that the cruelty and corruption of the human race can no longer touch them, because they know that they have nothing more to gain. Almost murmuring, they exchange question and answer with flat, muted, high-pitched expressionless voices – just the occasional glance, a smile, a tiny nod of the head: understanding. (*Theater Heute* 1970/13, p. 74. Quoted in *Peter Stein* by Michael Patterson)

This scene represents the essence of Bond's hope for the characters and his belief that Arthur's stand against the values around him can be communicated to Florence. It is not so much that a great director (albeit in an early production) has misrepresented the dramatist's intention; rather he has let the audience off the hook here by absorbing this strange and disturbing scene – Bond again describes it as a farce – into the all–embracing concept of his *mise en scène*. Bond is not interested in the possible dialectic created by a different mind interpreting his work. But his aim is precisely not to limit the scope of the production. He mistrusts other directors because he is well aware they are obliged, by reason of artistic integrity, to solve the play's problems. The value of a writer like Bond directing his own work is that he knows and can state how little the play actually answers.

In a recent interview on the topics of acting, directing and audience response Bond made the following remarks on his position as a theatrical craftsman. This definition of his aim and method can stand as a conclusion to the present analysis of his work:

I would like to feel there was some way in which you can dislodge segments of belief that people have so that the whole structure of their ideology is changed. Suppose there's a mosaic and I just move one piece. As a result of that every piece of the mosaic has to readjust itself. You can do that and end up with a different picture. That's a good approach to an audience. You might be knocking out cornerstones. Of course a whole mosaic can't be changed so easily. But you work at it because mosaics can be changed. This is a difficult experience for an audience and it should be an exciting experience. The audience should actually get a reward at the moment – but later they should get more. It should become part of the practice of their own life. (Interview with the author: 9th June 1984)

Chronology of Works

(Dates given are of the first performance)

The Pope's Wedding
9th December 1962, Royal Court Theatre.

Saved
3rd November 1965, Royal Court Theatre.

A Chaste Maid in Cheapside (adaptation)
13th January 1966, Royal Court Theatre. (unpublished)

Three Sisters (translation)
18th April 1967, Royal Court Theatre.

Early Morning
31st March 1968, Royal Court Theatre.

Narrow Road to the Deep North
24th June 1968, Belgrade Theatre, Coventry.

Black Mass
22nd March 1970, Lyceum Theatre.

Passion

Chronology of Works

11th April 1971, Alexandra Park Racecourse.

Lear
29th September 1971, Royal Court Theatre.

The Sea
22nd May 1973, Royal Court Theatre.

Bingo
14th November 1973, Northcott Theatre, Exeter.

Spring Awakening (translation)
28th May 1974, National Theatre.

The Fool
18th November 1975, Royal Court Theatre.

Stone
8th June 1976, Institute of Contemporary Arts.

We Come To The River (libretto).
12th July 1976, Royal Opera House, Covent Garden.

The White Devil (adaptation).
12th July 1976, Old Vic Theatre. (unpublished).

A-A-America (*Grandma Faust*; *The Swing*).
25th October & 22nd November 1976. Almost Free Theatre.

The Bundle
13th January 1978, The Warehouse.

The Woman
10th August 1978, Olivier Stage, National Theatre.

The Worlds
8th March 1979, Newcastle Playhouse.

Orpheus (ballet scenario).
17th March 1979. Wurttembergische Staatstheater, Stuttgart.
(unpublished)

Edward Bond

Restoration
22nd July 1981, Royal Court Theatre.

Summer
27th January 1982, Cottesloe Stage, National Theatre.

Derek
18th October 1982, The Other Place, Stratford-On-Avon.

After The Assassinations
1st March 1983, University of Essex. (unpublished).

The Cat (libretto).
2nd June 1983, Schloss Schwetzingen. (as *The English Cat*)

Red, Black and Ignorant
19th January 1984, The Pit (Barbican).

The Tin Can People
4th May 1984, Midland's Arts Centre, Birmingham.

Human Cannon
(for the Olivier Stage, National Theatre).

Select Bibliography

1. Editions of Plays

The order here is the chronological order of first performances listed above. If a work is not included here it is unpublished.

The Pope's Wedding published in *Plays and Players*, April 1969; London: Methuen, 1971; and *Plays: One* (incorporating author's revisions) 1977.

Saved published in *Plays and Players*, January 1966; London: Methuen (with Author's Note) 1966; *Plays: One* (with a new note to *Saved*, 'On Violence') 1977. New York: Hill & Wang, 1966.

Three Sisters (translation) published in the programme of the first production at the Royal Court Theatre, 1967.

Early Morning published London: Calder & Boyars, 1968; Methuen, *Plays: One* (incorporating author's revisions) 1977; New York: River Run Press, 1980.

Narrow Road To The Deep North published in *Plays and Players*, September 1968; London: Methuen, 1968; *Plays: Two* (incorporating author's revisions and with a new introduction: 'The Rational Theatre') 1978. New York: Hill & Wang, 1969.

Black Mass published in *Gambit*, vol 5 no.17, 1970; London:

Edward Bond

Methuen, (with *The Pope's Wedding*), 1971; *Plays: Two*, 1978.

Passion published in *Plays and Players*, June 1971 and *New York Times* 15th August 1971; London: Methuen, (with *Bingo*), 1975; *Plays: Two* (incorporating author's revisions), 1978.

Lear published London: Methuen, (with 'Author's Preface'), 1972; *Plays: Two*, 1978; Methuen Student Editions (with commentary and notes by Patricia Hern), 1983; New York: Hill & Wang, 1972; Chicago: The Dramatic Publishing Company, 1978.

The Sea published London: Methuen, 1973; reprinted (with 'Author's Note for Programmes'), 1975; *Plays: Two* (incorporating author's revisions), 1978; New York: Hill & Wang, (with *Bingo*), 1975; Chicago: The Dramatic Publishing Company, 1974.

Bingo published: London: Methuen (with 'Introduction') 1974; New York: Hill & Wang, 1975; Chicago: The Dramatic Publishing Company, 1977.

Spring Awakening published London: Methuen (with Introductions by Edward and Elizabeth Bond), 1980; Chicago: The Dramatic Publishing Company, 1979.

The Fool published in *Theatre Quarterly* vol.6, no.21, Spring 1976; London: Methuen (with 'Introduction' and 'Clare Poems'), 1976; Chicago: The Dramatic Publishing Company, 1978.

Stone published London: Methuen (with *A-A-America!* and 'Author's Note'), 1976.

We Come To The River published London: Methuen (with *The Fool*), 1976; 'We Come To The River Poems' also in *Gambit*, vol.68, 1976, and *New Writing and Writers*, vol. 13 (Calder), 1976.

A-A-America! published London: Methuen, 1976; reprinted (with 'Author's Note'), 1981.

The Bundle published London: Methuen (with 'The Bundle Poems' and 'A Note on Dramatic Method'), 1978; Chicago: The Dramatic Publishing Company, 1981.

The Woman published London: Methuen (with 'Poems, Stories and Essays'), 1979; New York: Hill & Wang, 1979; Chicago: The Dramatic Publishing Company, 1981.

The Worlds published London: Methuen (with *The Activists Papers*), 1980.

Restoration published London: Methuen – in the *Royal Court*

Writers series – 1981; revised version, 1982.

Summer published London: – in the *New Theatrescript* series – 1982; revised edition (including Poems, Fables and *Service*, A Story), 1982.

Derek published London: Methuen – in the *New Theatrescript* series – (with Choruses from *After The Assassinations*), 1983.

The Cat published London: Methuen (with *Restoration*), 1982.

2. Other Works

Theatre Poems and Songs edited by Malcolm Hay and Philip Roberts (London: Methuen, 1978)

'The Duke in *Measure For Measure*' plus a discussion with Harold Hobson, Jane Howell, Irving Wardle and John Calder in *Gambit*, Vol 5 no.17.

'Drama and the Dialectics of Violence': interview in *Theatre Quarterly* vol 11 no.5 (January-March 1972)

On Brecht': *Theatre Quarterly* vol VIII no.30 (1978).

'Us, Our Drama and The National Theatre': *Plays and Players* October 1978.

'*The Romans* and the Establishment's Figleaf': *The Guardian*, November 3rd 1980.

'The Theatre I Want' in *At The Royal Court* edited by Richard Findlater (Amber Lane Press, London, 1981)

3. Critical Works

Tony Coult: *The Plays of Edward Bond*. (Methuen, 1977)

Malcolm Hay and Philip Roberts: *Edward Bond. A companion to the Plays*. (T.Q. Publications, 1978) Revised version by Philip Roberts, (Methuen, 1985).

Richard Scharine: *The Plays of Edward Bond*. (Bucknell University Press, 1976).

Ed. C.W.E. Bigsby. *Contemporary English Drama*, Stratford-On-Avon Studies Vol.19, (Arnold, 1981) contains 'Edward Bond's Dramatic Strategies' by Jenny S. Spencer.

Theatre Quarterly Vol II No. 5 (January-March 1972) contains an article by Arthur Arnold: 'Lines of Development in Bond's Plays' and a Production Casebook of *Lear* by Gregory Dark.

Theatre Quarterly Vol VIII No.30 (1978) contains an article by Peter Holland: 'Brecht, Bond, Gaskill and the Practice of Political Theatre.'

Plays and Players November 1965 contains Peter Roberts's discussion with Gaskill, Cuthbertson and Johnstone: 'Three At Court.'

Tony Coult's article 'Creating What Is Normal' is published in *Plays and Players*, December 1975.

4. Other Works Cited

Bertold Brecht: *The Messingkauf Dialogues*, translated by John Willett, (London: Methuen, 1965).

William Gaskill: 'Brecht in Britain' in *Theatre At Work* edited by Charles Marowitz and Simon Trussler, (London: Methuen, 1967).

George Goetschius: 'The Royal Court in its Social Context' in Ten Years At The Royal Court: 1956-66 (published by the theatre as a souvenir programme 1966).

Pamela Handsford Johnson: *On Iniquity* (London: Macmillan, 1967).

Hans Werner Henze: *Music and Politics*, translated by Peter Labanyi, (London: Faber and Faber, 1982).

Eugene Ionesco: *Notes and Counter Notes* (translated Donald Watson) (London: Calder and Boyars, 1964).

Charles Marowitz: *Confessions of a Counterfeit Critic* (London: Methuen, 1973).

Michael Patterson: *Peter Stein* published in the 'Directors In Perspective' series, (Cambridge University Press, 1981).

George Bernard Shaw: *Man and Superman* in the Constable Standard Edition, 1903. London, 1931; and *The Quintessence of Ibsenism*, (London: Constable, 1891).

Index

173

Index